At Issue

Should Junk Food
Be Sold in School?

Other Books in the At Issue Series:

At Issue

Should Junk Food Be Sold in School?

Roman Espejo, Book Editor

GREENHAVEN PRESS
A part of Gale, Cengage Learning

GALE
CENGAGE Learning·

Farmington Hills, Mich • San Francisco • New York • Waterville, Maine
Meriden, Conn • Mason, Ohio • Chicago

Elizabeth Des Chenes, *Director, Content Strategy*
Douglas Dentino, *Manager, New Product*

For more information, contact:
Greenhaven Press
27500 Drake Rd.
Farmington Hills, MI 48331-3535
Or you can visit our Internet site at gale.cengage.com

For product information and technology assistance, contact us at

Gale Customer Support, 1-800-877-4253
For permission to use material from this text or product, submit all requests online at www.cengage.com/permissions

Further permissions questions can be emailed to permissionrequest@cengage.com

Articles in Greenhaven Press anthologies are often edited for length to meet page requirements. In addition, original titles of these works are changed to clearly present the main thesis and to explicitly indicate the author's opinion. Every effort is made to ensure that Greenhaven Press accurately reflects the original intent of the authors. Every effort has been made to trace the owners of copyrighted material.

Cover image © Images.com/Corbis.

LIBRARY OF CONGRESS CATALOGING-IN-PUBLICATION DATA

Should junk food be sold in school? / Roman Espejo, Book Editor.
    pages cm. -- (At issue)
  Includes bibliographical references and index.
    ISBN 978-0-7377-7189-3 (hardcover) -- ISBN 978-0-7377-7190-9 (paperback)
    1. School children--Nutrition--United States. 2. Junk food--United States. I. Espejo, Roman, 1977-
    LB3479.U6.S56 2014
    371.7'160973--dc23

              2014016065

Printed in the United States of America
1 2 3 4 5 6 7 18 17 16 15 14

Contents

Introduction

In July 2013, the US Department of Agriculture (USDA) released Smart Snacks in School, the final version of its guidelines for competitive foods. From sugary sodas sold in vending machines to cheesy nachos available à la carte, these are items offered outside of federally supported meal programs. Compliance with Smart Snacks in School went into effect July 1, 2014. To be allowed, according to the USDA, competitive foods must meet the following criteria:

- Be a "whole grain-rich" grain product; or

- Have as the first ingredient a fruit, a vegetable, a dairy product, or a protein food; or

- Be a combination food that contains at least 1/4 cup of fruit and/or vegetable; or

- Contain 10 percent of the daily value (DV) of one of the nutrients of public health concern in the 2010 Dietary Guidelines for Americans (calcium, potassium, vitamin D, or dietary fiber).[1]

Nutritional limits will also be imposed. For calories, snack items must have 200 calories per serving or less and entrée items 350 calories per serving or less. For sodium, snack items must have 230 milligrams or less and entrée items 480 milligrams or less. For fats, total fat must be 35 percent of calories or less, saturated fat less than 10 percent of calories, and zero trans fats. And for sugar, the limit is 35 percent or less of weight from total sugars in food.

Beverages that schools will be able to sell under Smart Snacks in School include plain water (with or without

1. US Department of Agriculture, "Smart Snacks in School: USDA's 'All Foods Sold in Schools' Standards," www.fns.usda.gov (accessed January 8, 2014). http://www.fns .usda.gov/cnd/governance/legislation/allfoods_flyer.pdf.

carbonation), unflavored low-fat milk, unflavored or flavored fat-free milk, and 100 percent fruit or vegetable juices. Juices diluted with water (with or without carbonation) must not contain added sweeteners. The sizes of beverages will be limited to eight ounces for elementary schools and twelve ounces for middle schools and high schools. "No calorie" and "zero calorie" drinks will be permitted for high schools, but must follow size limits depending on calories.

There are exceptions to these guidelines, however. They will not apply to competitive foods sold outside of school hours, on weekends, and at fund-raisers that take place off-campus. Furthermore, state agencies will be given the authority to allow on-campus fund-raisers to sell items that do not meet the standards or nutritional limits. "Based on feedback from nearly 250,000 parents, teachers, school food service professionals, and the food and beverage industry, we carefully balanced science-based nutrition standards, based on recommendations from the Institute of Medicine and the Dietary Guidelines for Americans, with practical and flexible solutions to promote healthier eating at school,"[2] declares Secretary of Agriculture Tom Vilsack. "We were able to achieve this goal while still giving schools flexibility to continue important traditions like fundraisers and bake sales, and preserve parents' ability to send in homemade lunches and birthday cupcakes," Vilsack explains.

Smart Snacks in School won some support for its potential to help change what children eat. A 2013 study published in the journal *Childhood Obesity* concluded that offering them healthier snacks in school vending machines or à la carte can positively influence eating habits. For example, the study found that schools doing so at lunch boosted daily fruit consumption by 26 percent, vegetables by 14 percent, and whole grains

2. Tom Vilsack, "A Healthier Generation Through Smart Snacks in Schools," USDA Blog, June 27, 2013. http://blogs.usda.gov/2013/06/27/a-healthier-generation-through-smart -snacks-in-schools.

by 30 percent. "When healthful food options are offered, students will select them, eat them and improve their diet,"[3] observes Katherine Alaimo, an associate professor of food, science, and human nutrition at Michigan State University. "Our study shows that schools can make the kinds of changes required by the forthcoming USDA guidelines, and these changes can have a positive impact on children's nutrition," she adds.

Nonetheless, Smart Snacks in School has been criticized for having loose guidelines for nutrition. "While in general the food guidelines are not bad and certainly an improvement, the sugar limits are especially lax,"[4] argues Andy Bellatti, a registered dietitian. "USDA is allowing foods with less than 35 percent sugar by weight, which is quite a lot. This means, for example, a product like Yo! Crunch yogurt with M&Ms topping 'passes.'" He also takes issue with the new rules on beverages, which he claims are "overly concerned with calories, while allowing diet sodas, diet iced teas, and diet juice drinks, without a care about the potential hazards of artificial sweeteners or dyes." Furthermore, Bellatti points out that foods with 0.5 grams of trans fats will be permitted because the figure is rounded down to zero. "[T]he presence of partially hydrogenated oils in a product should automatically disqualify it from being sold in schools," he maintains.

Smart Snacks in School is one of the sweeping changes brought to children's lunches since the Healthy, Hunger-Free Kids Act of 2010, which reformed the National School Lunch Program and the School Breakfast Program. These programs operate in more than one hundred thousand public and non-profit private schools and residential child care facilities. *At Issue: Should Junk Food Be Sold in School?* examines the elimina-

---

3. Layne Cameron and Katherine Alaimo, "Schools Help Kids Choose Carrots over Candy Bars," *MSU Today*, November 12, 2013. http://msutoday.msu.edu/news/2013 /schools-help-kids-choose-carrots-over-candy-bars.

4. Quoted in Michele Simon, "How Smart Are School Snacks? A Closer Look at New USDA Rules," *Huffington Post*, August 12, 2013. http://www.huffingtonpost.com/ michele-simon/how-smart-are-school-snacks_b_3744786.html.

tion and regulation of competitive foods as well as the introduction of healthy servings and options to menus and vending machines. The diverse commentaries, analyses, and reports presented in this volume represent the conflicting views on what children eat, why they choose what they eat, and how these choices can be improved.

1

Banning Junk Food in Schools Is Effective

Jonathon M. Seidl

Jonathon M. Seidl is deputy managing editor and founding editor of the Blaze, a news and media network.

Schools can succeed in enforcing a ban on junk food to promote healthy eating and fight obesity. In an economically struggling city in Illinois, Northeast Elementary Magnet School is transforming the lives of children and their families with its rigorous program and curriculum. In addition to its junk food ban, Northeast offers nutritious entrées and vegetables on the school menu, holds physical education each day, and requires parents to sign a "health contract," which instills students with healthy habits and ideals. Staff and teachers also set positive examples by shunning empty calories and actively participating with students in exercise. The school has won a prestigious award for its efforts, and has been credited with a promising drop in student obesity and attracting more families for enrollment.

Five-year-olds dance hip-hop to the alphabet. Third-graders learn math by twisting into geometric shapes, fifth-graders by calculating calories. And everyone goes to the gym—every day.

In the middle of America's heartland, a small public school, Northeast Elementary Magnet School, has taken on a hefty task—reversing obesity.

And it's won a gold medal for it, becoming the first elementary school in the country to receive that award from the Alliance for a Healthier Generation. The Alliance was founded by the American Heart Association and the William J. Clinton Foundation to reduce childhood obesity. Only two other schools have taken the gold.

The cafeteria here serves fresh fruit and veggies, low-fat or no-fat milk, no sodas or fried foods and no gooey desserts. There are no sweets on kids' birthdays and food is never used as a reward. Teachers wear pedometers and parents have to sign a contract committing to the school's healthy approach.

Northeast Elementary is not in some posh, progressive suburb. It's in Danville, Ill., an economically struggling city of 30,000 in farm country some 150 miles south of Chicago. But teachers, parents and students have embraced the rigorous curriculum and kids even call it "fun."

Northeast's strict, no-goodies program might sound extreme, but students seem to have bought it.

"We're a Healthy School"

From the outside, it's a drab 50's-era yellow brick building in a blue-collar neighborhood of modest frame homes, a few blocks from a homeless shelter and a Salvation Army donation center. Inside, it's a cheerful oasis for almost 300 kids and has caught the attention of some of the nation's biggest obesity-fighting advocates.

Former President Bill Clinton says the steps Northeast has taken are an exemplary way to tackle "a terrible public health problem."

"We will never change it by telling people how bad it is. We've got to show people how good it can be," Clinton said, paraphrasing a colleague at the Alliance's June awards ceremony in Little Rock, Ark.

Northeast's strict, no-goodies program might sound extreme, but students seem to have bought it.

During a recent nutrition lesson, first-graders sat raptly on the hallway floor as a teacher read "The Very Hungry Caterpillar," a classic kids' story about a caterpillar that can't seem to stop eating—all kinds of fruit at first. But when the bug moved on to chocolate cake and ice cream, the youngsters gasped and said in hushed tones, "junk food," as if it were poison.

"We're a healthy school," says 10-year-old Naomi Woods, a shy, slim fifth-grader. "We're not allowed to eat junk food or stuff like that."

Sandy-haired Timothy Mills, a fourth-grader, says the focus "just keeps us more fit, plus we have a lot more fun."

Like Mills, an earnest, heavy-set 9-year-old, Northeast kids aren't all skinny. Even some kindergartners are clearly overweight. But they still jump enthusiastically to the alphabet song, and though chubbier kids struggle to run around the football field during gym class, there doesn't seem to be much grumbling.

Physical education teacher Becky Burgoyne said it's sometimes tough to get kids of "all different shapes and sizes" to be physically active.

"I just ask that students do their best and improve on what they can already do," Burgoyne said.

Some schools "may have physical education twice a week, once a week, and that's not acceptable. Children need to move," she said. "To have a healthy body is to have a healthy brain and therefore they become better at reading and math and science. It all works together."

The students mostly mirror Danville and surrounding Vermilion County—generally poorer, less healthy than the state average, with many families struggling with obesity and related problems.

Learning Healthy Habits

The percentage of overweight kids at Northeast increased in 2009, the program's third year, but dropped slightly last year [in 2010], to 32 percent; 17 percent are obese. Those are similar to national figures, Principal Cheryl McIntire said. With only three years of data, it's too soon to call the slight dip in the percentage of overweight children a trend. But she considers it a promising sign, and there's no question that the children are learning healthy habits.

In a recent math class, fifth-grade teacher Lisa Unzicker explained how food labels can be misleading by listing only calories per serving, not per container. Pointing to an image of a pretzel bag label projected on a screen at the front of the classroom, she taught students to figure out how many calories are in a whole bag, based on the amount in each serving.

You have to be careful about potato chips and candy bars, she told the class. "This is why it pays to be a very conscious consumer."

McIntire is closely involved with choosing school menus and secured money from the state and local school district that have paid for fresh produce.

Teachers and parents credit McIntire for the school's success. The principal joined Northeast in 2008, a year after the staff moved to adopt the healthy focus, and has made it her mission to instill that mantra.

McIntire literally "walks the walk." When students need a talking-to, she walks to their classrooms and escorts them to and from her office rather than just messaging for them. When it's her turn for recess duty, she walks with her pedometer around the school's big field instead of standing on the sidelines. She recalls a student recently calling out, "Hey, Mrs. McIntire, are you doing your steps?"

McIntire is closely involved with choosing school menus and secured money from the state and local school district that have paid for fresh produce, including things like kiwi fruit that many children have never seen before.

A recent lunch menu featured whole-grain, reduced-fat cheese pizza, broccoli and cauliflower buds, sweet corn, chilled pears, low-fat pudding, and 1 percent low-fat milk.

McIntire has changed her own eating habits, giving up potato chips and shedding 15 pounds since last year.

Tall, slender and a youthful 56, McIntire guides Northeast with a firm but loving hand. She greets students by name each morning, helps with untied shoelaces, and offers hugs. And she scolds kids who have messy uniforms or are rude to their classmates.

School hallways feature signs about good food choices and being healthy, and a poster about the Alliance's gold award is prominently displayed near the school office.

"They Truly Stand Out"

The Alliance established a Healthy Schools program in 2006, with funding from the Robert Wood Johnson Foundation. It helps schools that want to become healthier and meet alliance criteria for winning medals. More than 500 schools have won bronze and silver awards. Those gold medals are tougher to come by. Memorial High School in West New York, N.J., was the first school in the country ever to win a gold. Last year, Northeast became the first elementary school to do that. Rio Hondo Elementary in suburban Los Angeles is the latest to win it.

Ginny Ehrlich, chief executive officer for the Alliance for a Healthier Generation says of Northeast, "They truly stand out." The school has done a remarkable job of making "healthy eating and activity the norm."

Since Northeast is a magnet school, students have to apply to attend, although they don't need to test in. Besides committing to the healthy mindset, parents must volunteer 26 hours at the school each year.

"There certainly are people who are much more invested than others, but we have gotten so much positive feedback from parents," McIntire said.

In her first year, McIntire recruited students by posting advertisements in the local newspaper. "I don't need to do that anymore," she said. For the current school year, there were more than 80 applications for 48 kindergarten slots.

"We have people calling everyday wondering if their child can get in," she said.

A Life-Altering Influence

Shelbi Black says Northeast has had an "amazing, life-altering" influence on her kids, 10-year-old Kayla and Carter, 5. They've come home requesting fruits and vegetables they used to reject. Carter was thrilled to make frozen fruit shish kebabs in school, and Kayla "was so excited the other day because she made her goal in running the mile and she was so happy that she knocked down her time from last year," Black said.

Tim Mills' mom, Charlyn Hester, says since the school adopted the healthy program, her family has switched from eating lots of convenience foods to lean grass-fed beef and lots of fruits and vegetables. Her oldest daughter, a recent Northeast graduate, has slimmed down and Hester says she thinks Tim and his 11-year-old sister will, too. Hester herself has lost almost 100 pounds since 2009.

The family's grocery bills are higher, but Hester, a freelance writer, says she and her husband, a security officer, have decided it's worth spending more on food and forgoing things like a new car, for their kids' health.

"It's not necessarily a financial hardship, but it's certainly an investment," she said.

Health department officials say they have not calculated obesity rates for children in Danville and the county. Psychologist Richard Elghammer, who works with a large rural health clinic in Danville, says about one-third of the kids treated there are overweight or obese—similar to the national average. National data suggest that the county's obesity rate alone for adults, about 32 percent, is also similar to the national average. About two-thirds of adults are overweight.

But Vermilion County rates of obesity-related illness including heart disease are higher, and more than 80 percent of county residents don't eat government-recommended amounts of fruits and vegetables, according to national surveys.

Dr. Thomas Halloran, an internist who treats adults in Danville, has been working to provide financial support and resources to Northeast, through his medical group, Carle Clinic. Halloran says many of his patients have diabetes and other illnesses tied to a lifetime of obesity and poor health habits. By instilling healthy habits in kids starting in kindergarten, the school is making an important contribution to the community's health, Halloran said.

2

Banning Junk Food in Schools Is Not Effective

John Metallo

John Metallo is a retired high school principal and former adjunct instructor at the University of Albany and the State University of New York at Plattsburgh.

From teaching and learning to bullying prevention and safety, schools have more important issues to address than monitoring the sale of junk food. What students choose to eat is the responsibility of their parents, especially since kids consume the majority of their meals at home or outside of school. Furthermore, offering healthy lunches and snacks does not mean students will eat them. In reality, most of the junk food eaten on campus is brought in. Trying to eliminate it from schools is a waste of time and money. Education begins at home, and parents should concentrate on teaching young children good eating habits.

I feel a lot better after reading the newspaper this morning. The federal government has banned the sale of junk food in schools across this great nation.

Finally, our schools will have something to do that is productive instead of worrying about things like teaching and learning, curriculum development, accurate budgeting, state testing, teacher evaluation, bus safety, sex education, character schools, bullying prevention, safety and security, psychological counseling, social work, health screening, etc., etc., etc.

Monitoring the sale of junk food in schools?

Give me a break, please.

What a waste of time and energy, from the Capitol building in Washington to the corridors of every school in the nation. This is simply something that is not the headache of the schools.

I worked in public schools for over four decades. And guess what? I really don't care what your kids eat. I don't care how much they weigh. I don't care if they develop lousy eating habits that will negatively affect them in future life.

How about the parents of these little cherubs of ours doing something instead of expecting the schools to raise their children for them? Schools would be a lot better off if we ask them to do what they are supposed to do—educate kids.

Schools are not meant to raise kids, nor will they ever be able to do that.

If schools serve healthy lunches, that does not necessarily mean that kids will eat them. . . . If there is junk out there, kids will find it.

Let's look at a few facts. Kids are not getting fat because of what they eat in school. They consume most of the food they consume at home or some place other than school.

Based upon a 180-day school year and three meals per day, a student consumes 180 lunches in school during a calendar year. That would move up to 360 meals per year if the student eats breakfast in school each day.

By the way, why are kids being fed breakfast in school? Shouldn't that meal be consumed at home in the presence of a caring and loving family? Given lunches only, a student would consume 180 meals in school and 730 other meals at home or elsewhere. That diminishes to 550 meals consumed outside the school for those who have breakfast and lunch in school.

Junk Food Is Not Going Away

If schools serve healthy lunches, that does not necessarily mean that kids will eat them. Some kids bring their own junk food with them from home. Some buy it from the corner store on the way to school. Some trade for it with their friends. If there is junk out there, kids will find it.

It is what kids do. Much more junk food is brought into a school each day than is sold in any vending machine in a school.

By the way, vending machines are in schools to help support things like sports and school activities, which are cut when budgets are slashed. If we properly fund those programs, we don't even need the vending machines. But that is another article.

We cannot expect our schools to solve all of the ills of society. How about we start taking responsibility for ourselves and our families?

Parents need to monitor what their children do every day. They should not expect the school or any other agency to do that.

Education begins at home. Teaching kids how to eat properly should begin long before the school years begin. Kids who eat healthy at home tend to eat healthy elsewhere.

Face it. Junk food is not going away. As a matter of fact, I like my chips on occasion. Trying to eliminate it from school or anywhere else for that matter is an abject waste of time and money.

Let's concentrate on teaching youngsters to make good decisions when it comes to food. That teaching begins at home.

Are you with me, Mom and Dad?

3

A Ban on Junk Food May Harm School Funding

Brian M. Rosenthal

Brian M. Rosenthal is a state government reporter for the Seattle Times, *focusing on social services, mental health, and public safety.*

A ban on selling junk food in vending machines at high schools in Seattle has dramatically reduced funding that student governments rely on. Permitting only milk, natural fruit juices, baked chips, and granola bars to be sold—items that have proven to be unpopular—student governments have lost hundreds of thousands of dollars in revenues, leading to costly increases in fees for athletic and student activities and the cancellation of programs. Moreover, many students have turned to convenience stores and gas stations off campus to buy junk food, which undermines the ban's mission to promote healthy eating. Given these impacts, the Seattle school board may relax the ban.

The Seattle School Board is considering relaxing its ban on unhealthful food in high schools amid complaints from student governments that the policy has cost them hundreds of thousands of dollars in vending-machine profits over the past seven years [to 2011].

The policy, approved in 2004—before any state or federal regulations on school nutrition had been established—put Seattle on the cutting edge of the fight against childhood obesity.

But board members now acknowledge they probably went too far. The restrictions, which are more strict than the now-crafted state and federal nutrition guidelines, allow only products such as milk, natural fruit juice, baked chips and oat-based granola bars.

Perhaps not surprisingly, many students are not particularly interested in those items.

In 2001, before the junk-food ban was passed, high-school associated student body (ASB) governments across the city made $214,000 in profits from vending machines, according to district data. This year, they've made $17,000.

The district promised in 2006 to repay ASBs for the revenue they lost because of the policy. But it never did. So the ASB organizations—which subsidize athletic uniform and transportation costs, support student clubs, hold school dances and fund the yearbook and newspaper, among other expenses—have had to cancel programs and ask students to pay significantly more to participate on athletic teams and in school clubs.

Students at some open-campus schools have made it a practice to walk to nearby minimarts and gas stations to buy the same products they used to purchase in the vending machines.

The impact has been especially hard on South End schools because most don't have wealthy parent groups to support activities and many students can't afford higher costs to participate.

Not Accomplishing Its Mission

Moreover, opponents of the ban on junk food say it's not even accomplishing its mission of preventing kids from eating unhealthful food.

That's because students at some open-campus schools have made it a practice to walk to nearby minimarts and gas stations to buy the same products they used to purchase in the vending machines.

"The kids will find the junk food," said Stephanie Ragland, a former PTSA [parent-teacher-student association] member at Franklin High School, which was hit especially hard by the ban.

Frustrated students, stung by dwindling ASB revenues, started discussing the ban last fall. The Seattle Student Senate formally passed a proposal to amend the policy last month and several students met with School Board members at a special work session Nov. 30.

At the session, Roosevelt High School junior Dexter Tang presented statistics about how the nutrition policy has impacted Roosevelt. He said the revenues from vending machines and student stores are down by more than $50,000 per year, and that's caused the school to cut back on funding to a range of student activities while increasing what have been called "pay to play" athletic fees.

Board members apologized to the students for failing to live up to their promise of refunding lost revenue. They said their tight budget makes it impossible to repay the money now, but they pledged to explore revising the ban.

"It doesn't make any sense at all," board member Sharon Peaslee said. "We definitely need to modify the policy so we can have all these new food and beverage possibilities in our schools and you can make money on them."

No members spoke in support of the ban.

That marks a stark contrast to 2004, when the board first adopted the policy. At the time, it was praised as a strong stand against unhealthful food.

Too Strong a Ban

But as school districts across the country (and state and federal governments) adopted less restrictive policies, it became clear the stand may have been too strong.

Former board president Brita Butler-Wall, who led the effort to enact the ban, acknowledged it went further than most other districts and hurt ASBs. But she said it still has a positive impact on students.

"It's very counterproductive to the educational mission to sell students stuff knowing that it's actually bad for them," said Butler-Wall, adding she opposes any revision to the ban. "I call it a tax on their bodies to fund the ASBs, and I don't think it's equitable."

Michael DeBell, the only current member who was on the board when the ban was approved, said that the board was well-intentioned but that "they went perhaps a little too far."

He said he supports revising the policy so it still supports nutrition but does not cripple ASBs.

"I think there's a middle ground," said DeBell, the board president. "I'd much rather see students buy reasonably healthy products in vending machines than junk food off campus."

District staff plan to present a proposal to revise the policy by next spring, with the goal of its taking effect next school year.

The revised policy is likely to match the state and federal guidelines, officials said.

4

Schools Can Find Alternative Funding to Junk Food

Marian Kisch

Marian Kisch is a writer based in Chevy Chase, Maryland.

Junk food in schools, also known as competitive foods as they compete with school meal programs, will be restricted by federal nutrition standards starting the 2014–2015 academic year. Competitive foods are commonly sold in fund-raisers and vending machines to support student and athletic activities, but the standards will not threaten such funding. First of all, switching to selling healthier food does not decrease revenues—sales rebound and total revenues generally increase due to the rising sales for regular meals. Schools can also participate in alternative fund-raisers, such as walkathons and other activities. And through various competitions, schools that excel at promoting students' healthy eating and exercise habits may receive grants and recognition for their accomplishments.

Elementary school students move past the fruit and vegetable bar, peering at the strange foods, pondering which ones to taste. There are 26 choices, one for each letter of the alphabet.

Twice a year at the Balsz Elementary School District's Health and Wellness Fair, students taste radishes, blueberries

Marian Kisch, "Competitive Foods in Schools: In Pursuit of Healthier Students, What Can Districts Do About Snacks and Beverages That Underlie School Fundraisers?," *School Administrator*, 70.7, August 2013, pp. 36. Reprinted with permission from the August 2013 issue of School Administrator Magazine, published by AASA, the School Superintendents Association.

and zucchini for the first time. And they're being introduced to fun facts about unusual foods such as jicama, kiwi, quince and Ugli fruit, all in an effort to encourage students in the Phoenix, Ariz., district to make healthier choices when they eat.

Candy, cookies, sports drinks and sodas are the food staples students expect to find available at their schools. But so-called "competitive foods"—the snacks and beverages sold in vending machines, school stores and snack bars and as a la carte items in cafeterias—soon will be subject to new federal nutrition standards. As part of the Healthy, Hunger-Free Kids Act of 2010, the U.S. Department of Agriculture [USDA] recently released the final nutritional standards governing the availability of competitive foods in schools.

The new rules are expected to take effect at the beginning of the 2014–15 school year, giving school districts one year to prepare. According to the Robert Wood Johnson Foundation, fewer than 5 percent of districts currently follow policies on the nutritional value of competitive foods and drinks.

School districts have taken various measures to introduce healthier foods. . . . Often these approaches have far-reaching effects.

A few school districts already have moved toward healthier options, both in their regular breakfast and lunch offerings, as well as in competitive foods. In part to deal with the obesity epidemic, these schools have eliminated vending machines completely or stocked them only with healthy snacks and limited beverage options to water, 100 percent fruit juice and low-fat milk. School stores in some districts no longer sell unhealthy foods, while their food service operations carefully monitor calories, sugar, sodium and fat content in the foods offered to students and reduce portion size. Salad bars are popular additions to cafeterias, while in-school fundraising events and school parties sometimes include restrictions.

AASA [School Superintendents Association] is one of several associations working with school districts in this effort. The Alliance for a Healthier Generation, which started in 2006 with 231 schools, now works with 16,000 to negotiate with food manufacturers to offer healthy snacks and beverages. The alliance also provides specific healthy food guidelines. The School Nutrition Association [SNA] offers training and resources, especially when new federal regulations are adopted. The Center for Science in the Public Interest has taken a stand on competitive foods and beverages, pushing for healthy granola bars, trail mixes and fruit cups in vending machines, while standing against high-calorie, sugar drinks and sports beverages.

The phrase "competitive foods" relates to snack foods and drinks that are sold in schools outside of the national school lunch and breakfast programs. The reason they are called competitive foods is because they compete with the school meals program, where foods must meet particular nutritional requirements.

Generational Poverty

School districts have taken various measures to introduce healthier foods, some writing new policies, others using gentle persuasion. Often these approaches have far-reaching effects.

Jeffrey Smith, superintendent of the Balsz schools, puts student wellness on the same level of importance as academics. "If kids are healthy, they will learn more and will be more successful," says Smith. He has tried to change people's viewpoints about healthy living in his high-poverty, rural district of five schools as a way to "change generational poverty."

Although the district has a basic written policy regarding competitive foods, the superintendent is working with AASA and the Arizona School Boards Association to develop a more comprehensive approach that will govern all aspects of snack foods and beverages on school grounds. Ultimately, he believes, this could be a model for the state and beyond.

In his daily work, Smith uses persuasion and collaboration to change individual behavior. "People don't do it because it's coerced, but because they feel it's the right thing to do. I don't want to have a written policy just so I can nail people if they're doing something wrong," he says.

Smith focuses on in-school food choices. Most Balsz schools are devoid of vending machines, except for staff lounges and those that sell bottled water. He seeks alternative ways to support athletic teams and other organizations that have been dependent on profits from sales in these machines.

When the superintendent noticed the student council at one school selling Popsicles after lunch, rather than unilaterally ban the practice outright, he spoke with the officers about other ways to accomplish their goals. Now students solicit sponsors for an exercise program, with the proceeds going to the council.

Over 50 percent of the calories that students consume are done so during the school day.

Smith also reaches out to the community to change unhealthy habits. He's started school/community gardens, arranged for food distribution four times a year at selected school sites in cooperation with the local food bank, educated parents at weekly talks and invited representatives from the local dairy council to speak to school audiences.

Balsz was recognized by the U.S. Department of Agriculture's HealthierUS School Challenge in 2012 for excellence in nutrition and physical activity.

One of the recognized schools, Griffith Elementary, has changed school practices to promote healthier eating and increased activity—breakfast in the classroom, a Food Day Fair for families and community members, and a weekly Zumba class for staff and families.

"At Griffith, better health and wellness support for our students, staff and community means better learning and behavior at school and better community relations," Principal Alexis Wilson says.

"This is a powerful way to change people's lives, but it's often overlooked in the busy life of a leader who has so many pressing needs every day," Smith adds. "But it is potentially life changing for these kids, who may live longer and be more successful. Embrace it and you can see powerful results."

Fueling Up

In Cabell County, W.Va., the high-poverty, rural/suburban district based in Huntington, with 28 schools, has been moving in the direction of healthier foods for several years. But it had a long way to go. In 2010, the Centers for Disease Control and Prevention named Huntington the unhealthiest city in the nation. Since then, the county and the state have enacted policies to restrict unhealthy competitive foods in public schools.

The school district introduced a program to encourage more physical activity by students. Several elementary schools participate in a walking program with the local hospital that includes health screenings and prizes. At Enslow Middle School, the West Virginia studies class "walked across the state," adapting lessons to the sites and history of the counties they traveled through. Enslow also sponsored a "biggest loser" contest among staff members over personal weight loss.

"Over 50 percent of the calories that students consume are done so during the school day," says Lisa Riley, Enslow's assistant principal. "That is why it is so important we do our best to manage these calories and make sure that we offer the most nutritious options possible."

Enslow students may purchase healthy products from vending machines directly before and after school, not during lunch. The school made the changes gradually, moving from french fries to baked fries and finally to sweet potato fries. The school offers taste tests of foods such as vegetarian chili or smoothies with spinach and other vegetables.

One popular addition at the district is the Fuel Up to Play 60 competition, sponsored by the National Dairy Council and the National Football League, to promote in-school nutrition and physical activity. "The idea is to fuel up with healthy foods so you can play for 60 minutes," Riley says.

Through the introduction of taste tests and a school walking club, Enslow earned more points in the Fuel Up Competition than any other school in the nation in 2011, receiving a $40,000 grant that was used to renovate the cafeteria and buy a $20,000 exercise system. The school has since added an indoor fitness trail and hired an after-school fitness coordinator.

Walking In, Candy Out

When Tony Swan became the principal at Fairview Elementary School in Klamath Falls, Ore., seven years ago, he found the school was selling chocolate bars and beef jerky sticks to raise money during the school day. He soon ended that practice, which he admits made club sponsors and booster groups nervous: "How were they going to raise money for the various activities they support?"

In reality, according to the National Alliance for Nutrition and Activity, schools do not lose revenue if they switch to selling healthier food. Initial revenue declines may occur, but sales rebound and total revenue increases at most schools because monies from the sale of regular meals increases. Also, most school districts typically keep only 33 percent of the funds collected from vending machines.

In the case of Fairview Elementary, Swan worked with the clubs on more acceptable alternatives. He suggested a walkathon, with students getting flat-rate pledges of $10 or more from family and friends. Now, once a year, all Fairview children walk around the high school track for 1½ hours to loud music and prize announcements. Parents and community organizations urge them on. Families join the walk, some pushing strollers.

To create even more of an incentive, Swan recently agreed to wear a chicken costume and do the "chicken dance" if students raised more than $4,000. When they generated $5,000, Swan donned a rented costume and gamely performed the routine while circling the track.

There's no use in offering foods students don't like and won't purchase.

Another elementary school sponsors a similar walkathon, and Swan expects additional schools to join in the coming year. The district is on board with these activities, as well as ensuring its competitive-foods policy meets strict dietary guidelines and nutrition- and fat-content analyses.

Food Ambassadors

School districts' food service departments sometimes come up with creative ways of including students in decisions about food offerings. Roger Kipp, who manages food services in the Norwood, Ohio, School District, established a student culinary council of 20 high school students, culled from leaders in their peer groups.

"They help us make decisions and changes as well as helping to educate and influence their fellow students," he says.

Kipp brings in vendors so students can taste the food and offer their opinions about what they like or dislike. The director admits there's no use in offering foods students don't like and won't purchase.

During the culinary council's meetings, which first ran weekly and now take place monthly, there's an educational component in which council members learn about nutrition, portion control, calories and other aspects of healthy eating. Whenever something new is to be introduced in the cafeteria, Kipp admits he'll proceed in an understated manner, something he calls a "soft" change. The students on the council will spread the word and explain why the shift is being made—for example, when spring rolls were about to replace french fries on the lunch menu. The students also pass out samples of healthy foods and encourage their friends to give it a try. They are the healthy-food ambassadors.

Improving the nutritional quality of a la carte foods also helps erase the stigma for low-income children who get free lunches and their wealthier schoolmates who are buying a la carte foods.

Stricter Policy

Larger school districts, such as the Chicago Public Schools, have a challenge in changing attitudes and behavior across hundreds of schools. In November 2012, the district adopted a strict competitive-foods policy for its 630 schools. District leaders solicited input widely, talking with parents, principals, students and community representatives, and delved into health guidelines, medical research and other appropriate resources. They were determined to improve their policy regardless of the new USDA guidelines.

Chicago's policy details what competitive foods can be sold. In vending machines, that means bottled water, 100 percent juice drinks and milk in containers of less than 8 ounces, are allowed. All carbonated beverages are banned. Vending machines, which are permitted in middle schools and high schools, contain snack foods that cannot exceed guidelines regarding fat, sodium and calories. School stores are prohibited from selling any food products during the school day, and a la carte options have been dropped from the cafeteria menu.

In 2012–13, 25 elementary schools piloted the new guidelines. Leslie Fowler, executive director of nutritional services in Chicago, insisted the healthier options worked. The pushback surprisingly came not from students but from some principals, who were leery about enforcing the new "cupcake policy," which allowed only two schoolwide celebrations a year involving snack foods. Even those educators now are on board, Fowler says, and the food services personnel, when asked, will attend parties and plan activities around healthy options.

A Healthier Future

The federal government's new competitive-foods guidelines, by all accounts, will be comprehensive and deal with the significant problems in children's diets today. According to Margo Wootan, director of nutrition policy at the Center for Science in the Public Interest, the guidelines are "in desperate need of an update."

She points out that improving the nutritional quality of a la carte foods also helps erase the stigma for low-income children who get free lunches and their wealthier schoolmates who are buying a la carte foods.

Sandra Ford, president of the School Nutrition Association, whose organization represents school districts' food service operations, believes offering healthy choices for students is the right thing to do, even though they can cause a drop in sales. In its response to the proposed USDA regulations, SNA has asked that the same rules regarding the nutritional standards of foods served in school breakfast and lunch apply to foods sold outside these programs.

"They should not impose a different set of guidelines," says Ford, who works as director of food and nutrition at Manatee County School District in Bradenton, Fla. For example, different definitions exist for fruits, vegetables and grain foods. The food service association wants both flexibility in what is served to students as a la carte items and accountability included in the policy. Once the new regulations are put into practice, the association will help its members adjust, Ford says.

Parents also are campaigning for healthier foods in schools. Ginny Ehrlich, former chief executive officer of the Alliance for a Healthier Generation, says, "Parents do not have control of what their children eat while in school, so they want to be assured they are consuming healthy foods."

The elimination of sports drinks from school vending machines may generate the most controversy. "They are pure sugar and don't belong in the school," Wootan says. "But lots of kids and adults don't realize this and think they are needed for physical activities. Not so. Water is adequate for hydration during the school day."

According to Ehrlich, studies show that students who eat breakfast at school perform better on tests and have fewer behavior problems. Those who perform better on state fitness tests also tend to get higher scores on state math and reading tests.

"We're seeing a culture change," she says, "where less-healthy options are being replaced with healthy foods and beverages. Everyone is buying into it."

5

Junk Food in Schools Contributes to Obesity and Threatens US Security

William Christeson et al.

William Christeson and the other writers of the following viewpoint are affiliated with Mission: Readiness, a nonpartisan and nonprofit national security organization of senior retired military leaders that promotes investing in the nation's youth.

With childhood obesity tripling in the last four decades, it is also the primary medical reason why people cannot enlist in the military: one in four young adults is too overweight to be recruited. Yet schools continue to sell junk food and sugar-laden drinks in vending machines. In fact, almost four hundred billion empty calories are consumed each year at campuses nationwide, countering efforts to serve healthy meals to students and teach children healthy eating habits at home, in addition to increasing obesity. Limiting junk food sales and improvements in nutrition, physical activity, and educating families have effectively decreased rates of obesity in numerous school districts, while also lessening the burdens of youth obesity on national defense.

An epidemic is spreading across the world.

The abrupt increase in obesity among American youth has set off alarms in America's medical community. Unfortunately many other Americans still are not aware of how rapidly childhood obesity has increased.

As reported in the *Journal of the American Medical Association*, 17 percent of girls age 12 to 19 years are now suffering from childhood obesity (not just excess weight). Even more boys in that age range are obese—20 percent—and the boys' rates are still rising.

Obesity rates are even higher among adults. In fact, one-third of all American adults are obese by the criterion used for adults: a Body Mass Index (BMI) of over 30, according to a survey by the Centers for Disease Control and Prevention (CDC).... While there has been a near doubling of obesity rates worldwide since 1980, no other major country's military forces face the challenges of weight gain confronting America's armed forces. Our male rates of being overweight or obese are higher than those of any other major country, according to an analysis by the World Health Organization. A different study in *The Lancet* further confirms that the U.S. has the highest BMIs for men and women, combined, among high-income countries.

One in Four Cannot Join the Military Due to Excess Weight

National surveys conducted for the military and by the CDC show that approximately one in four young adults is unable to serve because of excess body fat. When weight problems are combined with poor education, criminal backgrounds and other problems, an estimated 75 percent of all young adults could not serve in the military if they wanted to.

The Military Spends over a Billion Dollars a Year on Weight-Related Diseases

Because our country has failed to improve fitness and reduce obesity among our youth, the military has had to work much harder than in the past to recruit and retain enough qualified men and women who can effectively serve our country. For example, many accepted recruits are diverted to special training to address their inadequate physical fitness before they can even begin regular basic training. The costs add up. The additional medical expenses for soldiers on limited duty in the Army because of sprains or bone fracture injuries that are caused in part by some soldiers being less fit or overweight than other soldiers total half a billion dollars a year. The military's TRICARE health insurance system serves active duty personnel, their dependents and veterans. It spends well over $1 billion a year on treating weight-related diseases such as diabetes and heart disease. Many of those costs can be eliminated once America becomes more proactive in helping all its citizens to routinely become more active and consume less calories.

America's School Lunch Program Impacts Military Readiness

Following World War II, military leaders reported to Congress that, during the war, at least 40 percent of rejected recruits were turned away for reasons related to poor nutrition. This inspired Congress to establish the National School Lunch Program in 1946.

More than 60 years later, school nutrition remains a national security concern. In 2010, the retired generals and admirals of Mission: Readiness strongly supported passage of the Healthy, Hunger-Free Kids Act. This important legislation requires the U.S. Department of Agriculture (USDA) to update nutrition standards for all school foods and beverages, including "competitive foods"—those sold outside of school meal programs, in vending machines, in school stores and as à la carte items in the cafeteria.

As the Healthy, Hunger-Free Kids Act was making its way through Congress, Mission: Readiness issued the report *Too Fat to Fight*, which focused on the importance of providing healthy school foods. The Act had bipartisan support in both the Senate and the House and was signed into law in December 2010.

Since December 2010, the USDA has finalized regulations to update standards for school meals. The final standards will allow for more fruits and vegetables, whole grains, and low fat dairy products. The USDA hopes to finalize nutrition standards for competitive foods and beverages sold at school by the end of 2012.

Mission: Readiness applauds the USDA for its efforts thus far in updating nutrition standards for meals and looks forward to the finalized standards for competitive foods and beverages. We urge Congress to support the regulatory process and allow the USDA to finalize updated standards with input from nutrition experts and other knowledgeable experts on school nutrition policies.

School Junk Food Calories Equal More than the Weight of the Aircraft Carrier *Midway*

How is it that the amount of junk food sold to children at U.S. schools in a single year is equal, in calories, to almost 2 billion candy bars, more than the weight of the aircraft carrier *Midway?*

Children consuming an additional 130 calories in junk food sold at school each day is part of the obesity problem.

In 2005, scientists at the USDA conducted an in-depth survey of children's food and beverage consumption. They found that, on any given day, almost 40 percent of children in elementary through high schools—16 million children—consumed one or more competitive foods that were high-calorie, low-nutrient junk food, or sugar-sweetened beverages. These were foods obtained in school, but outside of the regular lunches. K-12 students who reported in the USDA survey that they were consuming high-calorie, low-nutrient food obtained at school averaged over 130 calories a day from these desserts, candy, chips, or other junk food, even excluding sugary drinks or sodas.

The 130 calories a day for all students consuming junk food equals almost 400 billion "empty" calories a year from foods low in nutrients and high in solid fats and added sugar. Our calculations show that those calories would equal nearly 2 billion candy bars, which would weigh almost 90 thousand tons—more than the weight of the aircraft carrier *Midway*.

National surveys on access to these foods, not actual consumption, conducted by the research program Bridging the Gap indicate that junk food and sugary drinks are still widely available to students in elementary, middle and high schools. The USDA has not repeated its consumption survey, but from the Bridging the Gap data on access to these foods and other data, it is clear that junk food sold in schools remains a major problem.

Exactly what do 130 calories per day from junk food mean in the long run for growing children? A study in the journal *Pediatrics* of child weight gain each year from 1998 to 2002 found that American youth consumed 110 to 165 more calories than they required each day. Over a 10-year period, those calories led to an excess 10 pounds of body weight for all teens. Clearly, children consuming an additional 130 calories in junk food sold at school each day is part of the obesity problem.

Children who are unable to buy junk food at school may seek to replace that food with other alternatives. The solution involves children consuming fewer empty calories inside and outside of school each day while eating more nutritious foods and getting more exercise. The bottom line, as many parents and nutritionists point out, is that we cannot succeed in teaching our children to eat healthier foods while continuing to sell junk food in our schools.

Getting Rid of Junk Food Is an Essential Part of What Works

Getting the junk food out of schools and serving nutritious school meals is both challenging and possible. It is unlikely that schools can successfully educate children about the need to improve their eating habits if the schools contradict that message by continuing to sell junk food. When New York City combined limiting junk food in its schools with other improvements in nutrition, physical activity, and child- and parent-education that took place not only in the schools but city-wide, rates of obesity among its K-8 children dropped by 5.5 percent in just four years. The younger the children the greater the decline in obesity. There was a 24 percent drop in rates of obesity among white 5- to 6-year-olds and 7 and 6 percent drops among black and Hispanic children that age—proof that large-scale public health change is possible in a short time frame and the earlier we make these changes in children's lives the better.

Studies show that decreased sales of junk food can be off-set by increased sales of regular school meals as kids buy more healthy meals.

Other places, such as Philadelphia and the state of Mississippi, are also starting to see meaningful progress in reducing childhood obesity.

An issue brief by the Robert Wood Johnson Foundation compared New York and Philadelphia, noting that, "In the mid 2000s, both cities implemented strong nutrition standards to improve the foods and beverages available to students." Philadelphia also improved school nutrition education, worked to make fresh fruits and vegetables more available in underserved neighborhoods, and had citywide public education campaigns to encourage healthier nutrition. Over a 4-year period, there was almost a 5 percent decline in the overall obesity rate for Philadelphia's K-12 students. The largest declines were observed among African-American males and Hispanic females.

The brief also highlighted progress made in Mississippi. Over a 6-year period, from the spring of 2005 to the spring of 2011, there was a 13 percent decline in the overall rate of overweight and obesity among Mississippi's K-5 students. The brief described the state's efforts to reduce obesity, including:

> "In 2006, the Mississippi State Board of Education set nutritional standards for foods and beverages sold in school vending machines. The Healthy Students Act of 2007 required the state's public schools to provide more physical activity time, offer healthier foods and beverages, and develop health education programs."

Progress made in New York City, Philadelphia and Mississippi suggests that removing junk foods and offering healthy foods at school is an important part of successful efforts to reduce childhood obesity.

Will Schools Lose Revenue by Eliminating Junk Food?

Some school districts have used profits from food sold outside of the regular school lunch program to fund their extracurricular activities and other school activities. Studies show that decreased sales of junk food can be offset by increased sales of regular school meals as kids buy more healthy meals. Instead of using their family's lunch money to purchase junk food on the à la carte line in the school cafeteria, or from school stores or vending machines, children will be encouraged to make healthier choices. According to a CDC review of the literature on limiting sales or junk food, "While some schools report an initial decrease in revenue after implementing nutrition standards, a growing body of evidence suggests that schools can have strong nutrition standards and maintain financial stability." For example, the CDC noted one evaluation finding that, "of the 11 schools that reported financial data, 10 experienced increases of more than 5 percent in revenue from meal program participation, which offset decreases in revenue from à la carte food service."

Reports from around the country reinforce the research. For example, the director of food and nutrition for Norwood School District in Ohio, Roger Kipp, eliminated vending machines and school stores in his district and created an area in the lunchroom where students could buy wraps, fruit or yogurt. He explained the eventual success of the change: "It took a while, but it caught on. You have to give the kids time. You can't replace 16 years of bad eating habits overnight." In New York City, a pilot program with special vending machines serving fresh fruit sells out almost every day and has to be restocked. According to Gerald Martori, principal at Benjamin N. Cardoza High School, "It was pretty much an instant hit."

U.S. Secretary of Agriculture Tom Vilsack has also reminded people to read the Healthy, Hunger-Free Kids Act: "It doesn't ban cookies. It doesn't ban bake sales." The Act is aimed at limiting the routine selling of junk food in school stores, vending machines or the cafeteria line.

The Risk Is Not Behind Us

The childhood obesity epidemic is still threatening our national security. In fact, the rate of obesity is still climbing among boys age 12 to 19 years. When the impact of the recession is over and fewer people seek to join the military, or if America is drawn into a new conflict, our military could again have trouble finding a sufficient number of well-educated recruits without serious criminal backgrounds, or excess body fat. Even among those who can be admitted, if they are physically unfit from a lifetime of nutritionally weak diets and lack of exercise, they will be more prone to injuries.

As retired admirals and generals, we know that America is not powerless in the face of this insidious epidemic. We do not have to keep surrendering ever more of our young people to obesity. We do not need to keep jeopardizing our national security because three quarters of our young people cannot serve in the military, a quarter of them because they are overweight.

Getting the junk food out of our schools is the obvious next step in our efforts to address the childhood obesity crisis. Congress should continue to provide bipartisan support for the process they approved to ensure that our children have access to more nutritious, lower-fat, lower-calorie food at school that includes fruits and vegetables, whole grains and lower-fat dairy options. These foods can help our children become strong and healthy. As a nation, we acted decisively to improve our children's nutrition after World War II and we should do so again.

6

Junk Food in Schools Does Not Contribute to Obesity

Jennifer Van Hook and Claire E. Altman

Jennifer Van Hook is a professor of sociology and demography and director of the Population Research Institute at Pennsylvania State University. At the time of press, Claire E. Altman was a sociology and demography doctoral student at Pennsylvania State University.

Schools are blamed for increasing childhood obesity and face pressures to eliminate "competitive foods" such as sodas, candy, chips, and other items from vending machines or snack bars. While competitive foods could increase daily calorie intake, arguments that their presence and promotion on campuses contribute to childhood obesity are naïve. For example, some evidence supports the idea that the structured school environment actually restricts opportunities for children to eat. Other studies find no significant weight differences between students attending schools with and without vending machines. Much of the evidence on both sides, nonetheless, remains inconclusive. To be effective, obesity interventions must extend their reach beyond schools to homes and communities.

Schools are often blamed for the production and perpetuation of widespread social problems and inequalities. Yet growing evidence suggests that we may be blaming schools for problems that originate in children's homes and neighbor-

Jennifer Van Hook and Claire E. Altman, "Competitive Food Sales in Schools and Childhood Obesity: A Longitudinal Study," *Sociology of Education*, vol. 85, no. 1, 2012. Copyright © 2012 by Sage Publications. All rights reserved. Reproduced by permission. Material has been edited for style, clarity, and length.

hoods, including the problem of childhood obesity. Here, we focus on the influence of "competitive foods" on children's weight. Competitive foods are sold in competition with the National School Lunch Program (NSLP) and the School Breakfast Program and include items such as soft drinks, candy bars, potato chips, cookies, and doughnuts. These foods are often sold in vending machines or snack bars and are not required to meet the nutrition guidelines for school meals established by the U.S. Department of Agriculture [USDA].

The calories from competitive foods purchased at school may replace, not supplement, calories consumed outside of school.

Over the past decade, pressure has been placed on schools to reduce or eliminate vending machines and the sale of junk food to children, and in 2006, the American Beverage Association pledged to stop selling sugar-sweetened soda in public schools. However, it remains unclear whether this focus on schools will reduce the prevalence of child obesity. Children's environments at home and in their communities may provide so many opportunities to eat unhealthy foods that competitive food sales in schools have little influence on children's weight. And, children may snack less at school than at home because schools structure children's time and activities, including meals. Although prior research has found associations between competitive food sales in schools and children's diet and weight, these studies are inconclusive due to reliance on small samples and cross-sectional data and limited attention to group variations in the effects of competitive food sales. . . .

Obesity and Competitive Food Sales in Schools

The percentage of overweight and obese children in the United States quadrupled during the past 25 years. The most recent estimates suggest that 35.5 percent of 6- to 11-year-olds are either overweight or obese, and 19.6 percent are obese. These trends are often attributed to the types and amounts of foods and drinks available to children, including those offered for sale in schools. Between 1994 and 2000, the share of middle schools selling soda in vending machines on school grounds increased from 61 percent to 67 percent, and the share of high schools doing so increased from 88 percent to 96 percent. These percentages appear to have increased even more in recent years.

Competitive foods sold in school could directly increase the calories children consume by increasing opportunities to purchase and consume energy-dense sweets, salty snacks, and sugar-sweetened beverages. Currently, soft drinks account for 20 percent to 24 percent of calories consumed by adolescents. On a 2,000-calorie diet, this amounts to between 3 and 4 cans of nondiet soda per day. And, soda and other sugar-sweetened drinks have consistently been found to increase the odds of overweight among children and adolescents and significantly contribute to the calories they consume.

Competitive foods may also increase children's weight indirectly through advertising, which could increase demand for soft drinks and snacks both in and outside school. Soft drink companies try to build lifelong brand loyalty by marketing to children in schools. Schools and school districts negotiate "pouring rights" contracts in which drink and snack vendors give schools upfront money (sometimes millions of dollars) and "incentive items" such as cups, T-shirts, posters, drink bottles, scholarships, and scoreboards in exchange for exclusive rights to sell their products in schools. Often, these contracts include specifications about the contents and placement of vending machines in high-traffic areas, hours during which vending machines are made available to students, and financial penalties for lower-than-expected sales.

But these arguments are somewhat naïve. They merely demonstrate the capacity of competitive foods to contribute to obesity. Competitive foods will not do so if children rarely purchase them. Additionally, the calories from competitive foods purchased at school may replace, not supplement, calories consumed outside of school. Despite pressure to restrict the placement, contents, and access children have to vending machines and competitive foods, the complete elimination of competitive food sales is controversial because of the lack of evidence of the harm of competitive foods and because many schools use the proceeds to build or buy sports facilities and equipment, furniture, sound systems, and computers and to fund scholarships or extracurricular activities. Several perspectives have consistently emerged in this debate. One position, the *external* perspective, is formulated from psychological theories about how people respond to food cues in their environment. An alternative idea derives from developmental models of how children develop food preferences and dietary patterns. . . .

Why Competitive Food Sales May Raise the Risk of Child Obesity

The external perspective posits that competitive food sales are likely to raise the risk of child obesity. The key idea is that children primarily consume the foods, either healthy or unhealthy, that are easily available or promoted in their immediate environments, regardless of their level of hunger or food preferences. This position is supported by laboratory studies showing that people will eat more food when it is visible and easier to obtain. In addition, several small-scale experimental or quasi-experimental studies suggest that children are responsive to food cues in school environments. One study examined changes in children's diets as they moved from fourth grade (when they only had access to school lunches) to fifth grade (when they also had access to a snack bar). They found that the children consumed fewer healthy foods and more sweetened drinks in fifth grade. Another study found that high school students were less likely to purchase food from vending machines when there were fewer vending machines or when they were operational for fewer hours. Finally, another study examined children's diets from three middle schools that replaced all snacks and drinks of low nutritional quality. Contrasted with children attending three comparison schools, the children attending the study schools reduced their consumption of junk food at school, with no compensatory increase at home. Additional evidence for the external perspective comes from a national-level study conducted by [researchers Patricia M.] Anderson and [Kristin F.] Butcher. Using an instrumental variable approach, they found that a 10 percent increase in the proportion of schools in the country that sold junk food was associated with a 1 percent increase in students' body mass indexes (BMIs).

Young, school-age children gain more weight in the summer months than during the school year, suggesting that influences in children's homes and communities are more important than school environments for the current childhood obesity epidemic.

Why Competitive Food Sales May Not Raise the Risk of Child Obesity

Alternative perspectives suggest that competitive food sales in schools are unlikely to influence children's weight. According to a developmental perspective, children may be relatively insensitive to food choices at school because their food preferences and dietary patterns were already well established in early childhood. If schools restrict children's food and drink choices, children may simply seek these foods elsewhere. Certainly, early childhood experiences and home environments have profound effects on children's dietary patterns. Some research suggests that children can lose the ability to self-regulate

food consumption (and stop eating when full) in early childhood, largely as a consequence of child feeding practices.
Daughters whose mothers are restrictive will eat more when
given the opportunity to eat forbidden foods than will other
girls. Another study showed a strong correlation between beverage consumption at age five and beverage consumption in
middle childhood and adolescence. Still another study showed
that children's weight trajectories between kindergarten and
fifth grade are largely explained by children's kindergarten
weight.

Constraints within school environments may further limit
the effects of competitive food sales on weight status. Schools
tend to exert much more control over children's time and activities than do nonschool environments. School days are
scheduled from beginning to end, including circumscribed
times for eating. Within a 15- to 30-minute time slot, children
eat at the same time in the same place with the same children
each day. This differs considerably from home environments,
where mealtimes are less regular, eating blends with other activities such as TV viewing, opportunities for snacking are
greater, and food consumption is less closely monitored, especially for children staying home alone. In general, situations
that fail to provide clear signals of when and how much to eat
often lead to "mindless" eating, that is, snacking without limit
and without recognition of the quantity of food consumed.
For example, adults eat more on the weekends when they
spend more time at home than on weekdays. So even if children consume unhealthy food from vending machines and
snack bars in schools, it is possible that schools structure
children's eating times so much that children do not have the
opportunity to go back for more, like they might if they were
at home.

Some evidence supports this idea. For example, children
appear to consume relatively little soda while they are actually
in school. One study based on an analysis of the 1994 and

49

1998 USDA food consumption surveys found that only 6 percent of soda consumed by children ages 6 to 17 was obtained from vending machines or school cafeterias. Similarly, [researchers Jason M.] Fletcher, [David] Frisvold, and [Nathan] Tefft analyzed fifth- and eighth-grade children in the Early Childhood Longitudinal Survey, Kindergarten Class (ECLS-K), and found that children attending schools with vending machines reported consuming more soda at school but the same *overall* amount of soda (consumed both in school and out of school) as children whose schools do not have vending machines.

Overall, these ideas about child development and school schedules shift the focus from schools to homes as the key environment that influences children's diets. The limited power of school-based competitive foods is reflected in empirical studies of children's weight. Fletcher et al. found no significant differences in BMI or the prevalence of overweight and obesity between children attending schools with and without vending machines, although their analysis was purely descriptive and did not control for other characteristics of children and schools. In a more rigorous analysis of the same data (ECLS-K), [researchers Ashlesha] Datar and [Nancy] Nicosia employed an instrumental variable approach to reduce bias due to the selection of heavy (or light) children into certain schools. They found no relationship between children's fifth-grade weight status and the presence or sale of competitive foods in their schools. Finally, [researcher Paul T.] von Hippel and his colleagues used the ECLS-K to examine children's weight gain between kindergarten and the end of first grade. They found that young, school-age children gain more weight in the summer months than during the school year, suggesting that influences in children's homes and communities are more important than school environments for the current childhood obesity epidemic.

The Current Study

These ideas raise important questions about the effects of competitive food sales on children's weight. Unfortunately, most of the evidence on this topic is inconclusive because, aside from a few studies, they do not adequately account for selection effects. As noted above, early childhood experiences and home environments have profound effects on children's dietary patterns. Heavier children may be more likely to attend schools with competitive food sales because parents who tend to raise overweight or obese children may also be less likely to pressure school administrators to eliminate the sale of junk food at school. . . .

The Need to Reach Beyond Schools

Schools seem to be natural places in which to enact cost-effective interventions. Because students are captive audiences, schools can communicate and interact with millions of children for extended periods of time. Schools also have the institutional capacity to coordinate and deliver consistent and well-defined interventions through an army of teachers and administrators. Yet, schools may not be good at addressing the root causes of childhood obesity that originate in children's homes and communities. Not only do we find that competitive food sales within schools are, on average, unrelated to obesity, but other research suggests that school-based interventions to reduce childhood obesity are often unsuccessful. Overall, schools may help promote better eating and provide opportunities for physical activity, but they do not seem to be effective at changing a student's weight. The challenge is to develop interventions that reach into the home and community. Perhaps those interventions can start with schools, but they probably need to reach beyond them to be effective.

7

Banning Soda Machines in Schools Will Reduce Obesity

Carol Duh-Leong

At the time of press, Carol Duh-Leong was a final-year medical student at Vanderbilt School of Medicine and on the board of Doctors for America, a nonprofit organization.

The increasing number of children who are overweight or obese is a national emergency. They face a higher risk of developing serious chronic conditions throughout their lives, including Type II diabetes and cardiovascular disease. The wide availability of soda and sugar-sweetened beverages has strongly influenced these troubling rates. For example, each can a child drinks per day increases his or her likelihood of obesity by 60 percent. Therefore, removing soda machines from schools will have a significant impact on childhood obesity. And unlike enforcing a tax on sugar-sweetened beverages, a ban on soda machines is less intrusive and has greater public support.

Overweight and obese children are at a higher risk of developing and suffering from the costly chronic diseases that walk hand-in-hand with a lifetime of obesity. For example, children who contract Type II diabetes are more likely to be susceptible to chronic conditions throughout their lives, including earlier onset of progressive neuropathy, retinopathy leading to blindness, nephropathy leading to renal failure, and cardiovascular disease. Recent research released this spring

[2012] has uncovered that Type II diabetes linked in obesity takes an even worse toll on these children than originally predicted, the disease "progresses more rapidly in children than in adults and is harder to treat."

This national emergency requires a multilayered approach. Here is one small peek into Tennessee.

Three short decades ago, one in ten Tennessee children were overweight. Today, this statistic has risen to one in every three or 36.5% of children in Tennessee are either overweight or obese, establishing Tennessee as the state with the sixth highest childhood obesity rate in the county.

Easy access to sugar-sweetened beverages has been a critical influence on childhood obesity. For each can of a sugar-sweetened beverage a child consumes per day, a child's likelihood of becoming obese increases by 60%. A 2004 study found that sugar-sweetened beverages are the single largest contributor of caloric intake in the United States, and accounts for 10–15% of caloric intake for children and adolescents. Targeting initiatives that reduce consumption of sugar-sweetened beverages is of paramount importance in the fight against childhood obesity.

Science suggests that a minor change in diet . . . will result in weight loss, making the removal of soda from the diet a concrete change that could deliver visible results in children.

The consequences of childhood obesity are alarming not only because of the disease burden linked to childhood obesity, but also because of the future devastation of how much it will cost to care for a majority obese adult population in Tennessee. As our country is struggling to control the cost of healthcare, the obesity epidemic will continue to demand higher costs. Federal studies demonstrate that obese children have a 70% chance of continuing on to become overweight adults. With over 30% of the state's population overweight or obese, Tennessee spent an estimated $1.57 billion ($355 per capita) on obesity related diseases last year [in 2011]—22% more per capita than the national average. This number is projected to rise to $7.08 billion ($1,442 per capita) by 2018.

There remains a pervasive belief that obesity exists because of an individual's lack of willpower or a lack of oversight on the part of parents when considering a case of childhood obesity. This misguided conviction stands as a barrier against championing sound public policy to counter this exploding epidemic. The obesity epidemic is one that cannot be treated in a doctor's office alone; it is the result of living in an environment where nutritious food is inaccessible due to an overabundance of non-nutritious foods through accessibility, affordability, and marketing rather than a matter of self-control. Public acceptance of this model is crucial to enacting policy initiatives that address these environmental factors.

A Concrete Change

Science suggests that a minor change in diet (reduction of even 100 calories a day) will result in weight loss, making the removal of soda from the diet a concrete change that could deliver visible results in children. There are several proposals on the table that aim to minimize access to sugar-sweetened beverages in Tennessee, including a tax across all sugar-sweetened beverages as well as a ban on soda machines in school.

Unfortunately, this single target is still quite complex. Many schools use the revenue from soda machines to fund school activities, making the removal of soda machines from schools a painful cut. One of the largest employers in Tennessee, Coca-Cola, maintains several bottling plants in the state. As a result of its significant investment in the state, the beverage industry has significant lobbying prowess in Nashville. Additionally, the beverage industry has invested billions of dollars to convince children that sweetened beverages are fun, athletic, sexy, popular, healthy, and even beneficial. Like the tobacco industry at the start of the anti-smoking wars, the beverage industry is preparing for war.

A policy directive should consider not only impact but also feasibility of the solution. Although a tax on sugar-sweetened beverages has the potential to reach a wider population, we must consider what policy measures are politically possible to achieve. Many state legislatures continue to discuss taxes on sugar-sweetened beverages as a reasonable method of combating the obesity epidemic (both directly from the effect on consumption and indirectly through the revenues generated), but the timing in Tennessee for such legislation remains complicated as the current recession environment is uncomfortable with new taxes. A public opinion poll revealed that a majority of Tennesseans (78%) opposed a special tax on snack foods. A more moderate approach may be more appropriate.

A Less Intrusive Solution

Like a scalpel is a more adept tool at demonstrating a clean result than a chainsaw, a ban on soda vending machines is a more elegant and less intrusive solution that has the potential for great effect on the lives of children in Tennessee. Public opinion on stricter school regulations is already beginning to turn positive: a slight majority (53%) opposed vending machines in elementary and secondary schools. Many schools have already begun to remove soda machines from their campuses on their own. In 2008, Tennessee ranked sixth in the nation for the highest number of schools that did not sell junk food (soft drinks, fruit juice that was not 100% juice, candy and baked goods) in vending machines, school stores, canteens, or snack bars.

Cutting vending machines may cut a source of funding for school activities. However, the disease ramifications of obesity are enormous and unless we take action now, we will approach a state and national emergency. Revenue from soda is no longer an appropriate source of funds, the way that revenue from cigarette machines would not be [an] appropriate source of funding. We must shoulder the responsibility to build an environment for our children that is nutritious and healthy. The consequences otherwise, are just too heavy.

8

Eating Healthy Foods During Short Lunch Periods Is Hard for Students

Joanna Lin

Covering K–12 education, Joanna Lin is a data reporter for the Center for Investigative Reporting, a nonprofit journalism organization.

Changes in federal nutrition standards require schools to serve students more fruits and vegetables at lunch. However, many students lack the time to eat them. Serving hundreds of meals at once within tight instructional schedules, schools nationwide are failing to provide the recommended minimum of twenty minutes to eat lunch. The average lunch period is thirty-one minutes, but students may wait up to thirty minutes to be served, according to recent data. Some schools are devising ways to give them more time to eat, such as deploying extra staff and installing vending machines with full meals. Still, many students say they face long lines and waits.

The green beans are portioned and displayed in orderly rows. The lasagnas are steaming up their plastic covers. The workers stand ready, their hair netted and aprons tied. The bell rings, and a stream of nearly 1,000 students flood in to Francisco Bravo Medical Magnet High School's cafeteria, barely slowing as they load cardboard trays with apple juice, chicken wings and sliced cucumbers.

Because lunch is free for all students at Bravo, in the Boyle Heights neighborhood of Los Angeles, no one pauses to pay. Still, during the lunch rush this day in May [2013], food service worker Rodelinda Gomez stops a few.

"Hey! Hey!" Gomez hollers to students with no greens on their trays. "Come on and get your vegetables. You have to get them!"

For schools to receive federal reimbursement for lunches, they must serve—not just offer—each student at least a half-cup of fruit or vegetables. Lunches also must include servings of at least two other foods, such as a protein and a grain.

More Time than Many Students Have

The requirement, adopted in the last school year, is part of an effort to serve students healthier foods. And eating those foods takes time—more time than many students have.

"A student can eat a cup of apple sauce in no time—you can practically drink that. But chewing through an apple takes a lot longer," said Diane Pratt-Heavner, spokeswoman for the School Nutrition Association, a national advocacy organization. "If we want our students to eat more salads, fruits and vegetables, we need to give them more time to consume them."

National school and health organizations and some states—including California—recommend that students have at least 20 minutes to eat lunch after they're served. But "that's not happening in all schools," Pratt-Heavner said.

Uneaten meals mean hungry students who are more prone to headaches, stomachaches and behavior problems and less able to concentrate in class.

Nationwide, the average lunch period was 31 minutes in the 2009–10 school year, according to the U.S. Department of Agriculture's most recent data available. Students waited in line an average of five minutes and as long as 30 minutes to get lunch, food service managers reported.

The Los Angeles Unified School District has touted the 20-minute standard since 1990. Yet a district analysis last year showed that 7 out of 10 high schools and nearly half of elementary schools missed the mark.

"What we find is, with the kids that don't have the time, they don't eat anything," said David Binkle, the district's director of food services.

Trying to Carve Out More Time to Eat

Uneaten meals mean hungry students who are more prone to headaches, stomachaches and behavior problems and less able to concentrate in class, educators say. They also increase food waste.

Last year, L.A. Unified's school board reaffirmed its policy to provide all students enough time to eat. As students return to campus this month, many will see more lunch lines, points of sales or staff to serve them; others will have longer lunch periods, Binkle said.

By the end of the school year, Binkle hopes to have cut in half the number of schools failing to offer at least 20 minutes to eat lunch.

Advocates say L.A. Unified is the only district they know of that's trying to provide students a minimum time to eat.

"I don't think (it) is on our radar for any of the other districts. Not that it's not needed—it's just so difficult," said Nicola Edwards, a nutrition policy advocate at California Food Policy Advocates.

Across California, schools face a number of challenges in carving out enough time to eat.

Aging facilities can mean cramped cafeterias and long lines. And tight bell schedules that prioritize instructional minutes leave lunchtime with "the short end of the stick," said

Joanne Tucker, food services marketing coordinator for the San Diego Unified School District.

Still, there are ways schools are trying to allow students more time to eat.

When lines get too long, the San Jose Unified School District deploys extra staff to help serve lunch, said John Sixt, the district's director of student nutrition.

The San Francisco Unified School District is piloting vending machines that sell full meals, allowing students to skip the cafeteria, said Zetta Reicker, the district's assistant director for student nutrition services.

San Diego Unified used grant money to roll out mobile food carts at its high schools, creating more places to get food on campus. At San Diego High School, where 2,700 students attend five smaller thematic schools, there are 22 service locations.

Some advocates say quick, portable meals are a step in the wrong direction.

Waits Can Still Be Too Long

But even with multiple service locations, students say waits still can be too long.

Randy Saelee, now a senior at Oakland High School, said he decides what to eat based on which of the school's seven service areas has the shortest line. The Friday before school let out for summer, a horde of students blocked his view of his chosen cafeteria window.

"I guess tacos?" he said with a shrug.

Even with this approach, Saelee said he typically waits 20 to 25 minutes because people cut in line.

At Oakland High, students punch in their ID numbers, so that staff can track free and reduced-price meals in one line and then receive tickets they'll exchange for lunches in other lines.

"There's never enough time," said Yvette Santos, who graduated in June. "You have to get in a line to get a ticket, then get into another line to get the food. Then your food's cold when you get it."

Schools short on time often serve grab-and-go meals and preportioned foods. Both options can be found at Bravo in Los Angeles, which has a 30-minute lunch period and serves 1,000 lunches per day.

As many as 200 students ate grab-and-go lunches when they took standardized tests this spring and could not leave their classrooms, said Bob Milner, the school's cafe manager. The meals are also a popular choice for students who have tutoring or club meetings during lunch.

Steps in the Wrong Direction

Some advocates say quick, portable meals are a step in the wrong direction.

"It's really not what we want to teach children to do—to grab their food and eat it in the car or eat it on the run," said Zenobia Barlow, executive director of the Center for Ecoliteracy, which has advocated for school food reform. "To get a healthy meal and sit down and just eat it like a human being—(it) seems like we really need to take a look at that and try our best to preserve some quality in that experience."

To Sharelette Rodgers, a food services manager for Oakland Unified, time is not a problem. "The kids would just rather go to the fast food places," she said.

Or, they would rather not eat at all. "Sometimes, I don't eat because I don't like it," Cedric Bonsol, now a junior at Bravo, said of school lunches.

In school after school, the primary complaint students have about lunch is not the time but the food itself. Binkle, of L.A. Unified, said the issues are related. He likened the school cafeteria to a restaurant trying to serve 2,000 meals in 20 minutes.

"If you had 40 minutes, then we'd only have to prepare half and serve half at a time," he said. "You get much higher-quality food, you get much fresher food, because it's being cooked more to order than ... scrambled eggs on the buffet that have been sitting there for six hours. The longer you stretch it out, the more personalized the service and the quality of food is improved."

9

Healthy, Organic, and Cheap School Lunches? Order Up

Greg Toppo

Greg Toppo is an education reporter for USA Today.

Serving wholesome meals to millions of students within budget in the nation's schools remains a challenge. The federal government spends less than $3 per child per meal, and $5 is touted as necessary to provide natural and fresh, not processed or canned, foods. However a small company is successfully delivering locally sourced, organic breakfasts and lunches—free of high-fructose corn syrup, artificial additives, trans fats, deep frying, hormones, and antibiotics—to hundreds of schools for under $3 apiece. Some commentators question the nutritional advantages of the meals and sustainability of the company's business model, but participating schools attest to the positive impacts on students' diets and academic performance.

On the combination plate of problems plaguing the USA's public schools, few are as intractable as this. Can you serve fresh, healthful meals each day to millions of kids without breaking the bank, or must you resort to serving up deep-fried, processed, less expensive junk?

For more than a decade, big food thinkers have chewed on this, making it a cause célèbre. But most often they find that feeding kids well requires one simple thing: more money.

The federal government pays, on average, $2.68 per child per meal—and most food advocates say that simply isn't enough. A few insist it can't be done for less than $5.

So it's big news when someone tries, even on a small scale, to feed kids well for under $3 a pop.

An All-Natural Meal

For the first time, a small, privately held start-up is pushing to do just that: producing what are by all accounts fresh, healthful, all-natural school meals for just under $3 apiece. Starting with just one school in spring 2006, Revolution Foods has quietly grown year by year and now delivers about 45,000 breakfasts, lunches and snacks daily to 235 public and private schools in California, Colorado and the District of Columbia.

Revolution shuns high-fructose corn syrup, artificial colors and flavors, trans fats and deep-frying.

Since April [2009], about 14,000 of those meals each day have come from a 22,000-square-foot facility in an Oakland industrial park.

The growth is impressive, but what's perhaps most striking is what the meals look and taste like—and the rogues' gallery of components (fries, canned green beans, cling peaches in heavy syrup) that are missing.

Revolution shuns high-fructose corn syrup, artificial colors and flavors, trans fats and deep-frying. Its meats and milk are hormone- and antibiotic-free, and many of its ingredients are organic and locally sourced.

Company co-founder and chief operating officer Kirsten Saenz Tobey says Revolution's plan is to "take the school lunch problem off the schools' plates" with kid-friendly but healthful food. "A principal doesn't want to manage a restaurant."

Margo Wootan, nutrition policy director for the Center for Science in the Public Interest, says she's slightly concerned with Revolution's insistence on natural, local ingredients.

"You can have full-fat cheese from a local farmer, and it's still going to clog your arteries and give you heart disease," she says. "Having the food be natural is nice, but a bigger threat to children's health is making sure that there's not too much salt and not too much saturated fat."

Banishing high-fructose corn syrup, Wootan says, is "a waste of time and money"—better to limit children's total sugar intake. As for hormone-free milk, she says, most milk is hormone-free. "And if it isn't, it's not a health problem."

A Sustainable Model?

Much of Revolution's success has come from its ability to lower food costs by cutting deals with a handful of suppliers.

"They see us as a great distribution channel," Tobey says. "In one day we'll produce 30,000 turkey sandwiches—that's a lot more than is sold in a grocery store."

Katie Wilson, former president of the School Nutrition Association and nutrition director for the Onalaska, Wis., school district, admires Revolution's push to offer whole foods at a lower cost but says she's not sure it's a sustainable national model.

"Their suppliers are giving them a break now because it's quite popular to be in the market for school meals," she says. "How long will suppliers continue to give them a break?"

Revolution isn't the first to give this a try. In the past several years, several high-profile chefs have pushed to reinvent school lunch.

Just last month, Food Network star Rachael Ray got into the game, partnering with New York City public schools to develop a new menu and "get kids excited about the food they eat while embracing a healthier lifestyle."

The move to reinvent school lunches reflects new recommendations from the federal Institute of Medicine, which said last month that schools should limit sodium and calories and encourage children to eat more fruits, vegetables and whole grains. Even the institute says the recommendations "will likely raise the costs of providing school meals." In his 2010 budget, President Obama asks for an additional $1 billion for the school lunch program.

Thea Stewart, a kindergarten teacher at KIPP DC: LEAP Academy, a charter school in Southeast Washington, D.C., says most of her students get most of their daily nutrition from Revolution: breakfast, lunch and snacks.

She says the company's attention to healthful menu items makes a huge difference in her students' abilities to concentrate.

"I think the food is a contributing factor to that," Stewart says. "It is not a lot of sugar and not a lot of heavy food."

No Canned Response

At a recent in-classroom lunch session at LEAP Academy, barbecue turkey and cheese wraps, sealed in little cardboard trays, are on the menu. U.S. Agriculture Department rules say all meals must include vegetables and fruits, but for many students, that means canned fruits and vegetables. Here, students find fresh lettuce and tomatoes in their wraps and, as they settle in, Stewart and a co-teacher offer each student a tiny green pear or yellow apple.

Morgan Bailey, 5, pops open the cellophane wrapper on her lunch and suspiciously eyes the little container of light brown dipping sauce. She nibbles the wrap for a few moments without touching the sauce. Then, at an adult's urging, she delicately dips a corner into the container and gives it a taste. Not bad.

Tobey is tight-lipped about the company's plans to expand to other markets but says, "It's likely that we will."

In the meantime, she and her partner, Kristin Richmond, an investment banker, are in high demand to talk about their business model.

"We are really happy to share as much as we can about what we do," she says, but she warns that Revolution has stayed fairly small for a good reason.

"It's not really something that's easy to replicate," she says. "If somebody can figure out what we're doing on a bigger scale, more power to them."

10

Schools Depend on Snack Sales to Keep Cafeterias Solvent

Mary Beth Pfeiffer

Mary Beth Pfeiffer is a Pulitzer Prize–nominated investigative reporter for the Poughkeepsie Journal.

Despite the alarming numbers of children who are now over-weight or obese, public schools continue to sell unhealthy snacks, beverages, and other "competitive foods" because of the sizable income they earn. Ironically, schools depend on these sales to subsidize recent federal regulations for expensive fruits, vegetables, and lower-fat items to be served in school lunches. An investigation of several school districts in New York State demonstrates that competitive foods generate large amounts of revenue, while mandates for servings of whole grains, fruits, and vegetables have significantly increased costs and tightened budgets. Federal regulations announced in June 2013 will impact competitive foods, but many food managers worry that they will not be effective or fear a total ban on such profitable items.

While raw carrots call out for takers at a local school cafeteria, the line for the snack window is 10-deep with sixth-graders awaiting frosted zebra cakes, fried dough sticks and many more sugar- and fat-laden treats.

Why does Highland Middle School offer such junk food?

"Purely for money," said Maria McCarthy, food service director for the district, which sold $52,000 in vending machine items and $189,000 in so-called a la carte foods and snacks in 2011–12, among them a high school favorite, nachos with cheese.

About one-third of public school children locally are overweight or obese—some district rates top 40 percent—and the numbers are rising to levels that one local pediatrician called "appalling." Yet public schools sell sometimes-unhealthy snacks and fatty alternatives to balanced, government-regulated lunches for a simple reason: They earn hundreds of thousands of dollars, according to an exclusive *Poughkeepsie Journal* review of financial documents and menus and interviews with food service managers.

Ironically, schools need this income to fill growing holes in their food service budgets, the *Journal* found, as regulations require them to serve healthier—and expensive—fruits, vegetables and lower-fat foods with government-approved lunches. Further, new regulations effective in the 2014–15 school year will sharply restrict the sale of the sugary, fatty and salty delights that go head-to-head with healthier fare—and will undoubtedly compound the financial problem.

All school districts raise money on what are called "competitive foods," though some sell more than others.

The 16 districts brought in more than $5 million, or 27 percent of revenues, on sales of snacks, lunch and breakfast food . . . that would not pass muster under the meal guidelines of the National School Lunch Program.

The biggest earner by far was Arlington, which hauled in more than $2 million in the 2011–12 school year on an extensive menu of pizza, nachos, chicken nuggets, salads and french fries.

In Millbrook, snack and a la carte foods brought in an estimated $73,000 in the 2012–13 school year. Poughkeepsie schools earned $224,000 in 2011–12, about a tenth of food revenue. Hyde Park got $130,000 from vending machines alone that year, while Dover schools raised $90,000 from sales of things like Yoo-hoo, Gatorade, ice cream and cookies.

The 16 districts brought in more than $5 million, or 27 percent of revenues, on sales of snacks, lunch and breakfast food—bacon-egg-and-cheese bagels, for example—that would not pass muster under the meal guidelines of the National School Lunch Program. (Some revenues came from sales of milk, staff meals or seconds on milk and nutritious lunches.)

Better Foods Sold

Not all school snack and a la carte foods are of the junk food genre. Many districts—such as Red Hook, Poughkeepsie and Dover—offer salads and chopped vegetables, while selling lower-sugar drinks and lower-fat potato chips and ice cream. But many packaged snacks aren't nutritious either, experts say, and—as is clear in Arlington—they and their ilk compete with healthier lunches, which today must include fresh fruits, vegetables and low-fat milk.

Sales of snack foods in schools surely aren't the only cause of a scourge of childhood obesity in a fast-food, on-the-go society. But evidence suggests they contribute. A 2005 study by the National Bureau of Economic Research, a nonprofit research organization, concluded: "Availability of junk foods in schools can account for about one-fifth of the increase" in child size over a decade.

The need for better nutrition while paying the bills has put school cafeterias in a bind. Food programs were mandated this past year to offer whole grains and fresh fruits and vegetables, with limits on portions of meat and grains; the changes led to a drop in sales in many local districts even as costs rose. The cost of produce rose in Arlington schools from

$50,000 to $90,000, for example. As a result, cafeterias have become even more dependent on the sale of chips and treats to fill deficits, which for all districts totaled $797,000 in the *Journal*'s study.

"It's sad we have to do this," said Walter Robinson, lunch manager for Millbrook schools, which sells foods he admits are not good for children: pre-fried mozzarella sticks, nachos with cheese, ice cream sundaes and chocolate chip cookies. "I would love to be able to make ends meet or make budget by just selling healthy lunches." Many other managers agreed.

Food programs are ostensibly independent businesses within schools, reliant on two primary revenue streams: reimbursements under the National School Lunch Program for children who receive free and reduced-price lunches, and sales of food. Those sales include approved meals for students who pay full price, second helpings on them, and the always popular a la carte foods and snacks. The federal program reimburses schools $2.86 for meals to children who pay nothing; $2.46 for reduced-fee lunches and 27 cents for full-price meals.

Like many other food directors, Dover's Marilyn Serino said, "The other sales are necessary to offset the cost of meal production." Government aid and meal sales, she said, do "not even begin to cover" program costs, among them more than $100,000 this year in health insurance for seven food workers.

"Lesser Evil"

Keenly aware of growing childhood obesity—and related problems like Type 2 diabetes—many food managers profess to offer healthier snacks. Water is a snack staple in many schools along with reduced-fat chips; several food managers boasted their deep fryers were long retired. But some districts limit their offerings more sharply than others, and some new products in many schools might better fall into a lesser-evil rather than healthful category.

Among those offered locally: a single-serving Pop-Tart, one-ounce bags of reduced-fat Doritos, mini-Rice Krispies Treats, lower-sugar coconut water (in 20-ounce bottles) and lower-fat cheese crackers.

[School districts] say they need to make ends meet by selling food to kids, some of it junk.

Hyde Park offers Gatorade with one-third of the sugar. Dover offers baked Cheetos (alongside hot Buffalo wing potato chips). Arlington sells bite-size servings, including 1 1/2-ounce brownies and 3-ounce muffins.

"I think it's a double-edged sword," said Clara Wittek, Red Hook's food service director. "To a certain extent, it is a lesser evil. To a certain extent, it does help the program. . . . Let's face it—a dollar is a dollar."

Though some districts undoubtedly draw a tougher line on snack foods, all face the same quandary: They say they need to make ends meet by selling food to kids, some of it junk.

"The driving force behind most of the decisions in this school district is, 'Can we afford it?'" said McCarthy, food director at Highland. "We're at the tipping point." For 2012–13, the district kicked in $70,000 to run the food service, which exhausted its $1.2 million budget two months before the school year's end, in part because of falling sales and more expensive food, officials said.

Indeed, 11 of 16 meal programs surveyed by the *Journal* needed a budget stipend from their school district—of $15,000 to $115,000. The remaining five that got no district money ran deficits that signal future problems.

Said Carol Beebe, executive director of the New York School Nutrition Association: "I see my members and I ask them, 'How's it going?'" she said. "They're all losing money."

This is where that 65-cent bag of cheddar popcorn or 75-cent Sunny Delight comes in. Kids like them; they buy them.

"There's kids that eat this instead of lunch," said Stacey Malheiro, a kitchen worker who was doing a brisk business in June in Nutty Bars and Little Debbie confections at the Highland Middle School snack stand. "It kills me as a mother."

Some children in the district are so overweight that they struggle to walk the stairs or participate in gym, she said. In Highland, 19 percent of students are obese, state statistics show.

New Rules Loom

Though school lunches underwent major changes last September—in which fats and calories were reduced—school snacks long have been all but unregulated. In New York, soda, gum, hard candies and non-fruit ices were banned for sale during school hours in 1987.

And while 39 states have some limits like New York's, the federal school lunch program long has had a hands-off policy on "competitive foods." Federal regulations released in June will change that as of September 2014, and local managers are bracing for a budget hit. But some nutrition advocates fear the changes, already reflected in some local offerings, will not be nearly as comprehensive and meaningful as necessary.

"Reduced-fat corn chips and baked potato chips are still junk foods with almost zero nutritional value," wrote the Center for Food Safety, a Washington, D.C., nonprofit, in commenting on the proposed regulations. "The fast food, soft drink, and junk food companies are happy to comply with minor tweaks to their products to ensure their brands remain in schools." The center argued instead for a total ban on non-meal foods.

"Wouldn't it be great if we could stop selling snacks," said Abraham Nuchman, school lunch director for 14 schools in the Wappingers district. "That's what we all want to see happen."

But he and other local managers fear that would lead to financial ruin. The lost revenue would force them to raise the cost of nutritional meals as the federal program is pressuring them to do. But that has led to a loss of paying customers in many districts, where lunches range from $2.40 in Kingston, for example, to $3.25 in Rhinebeck.

Such pressures might force some districts to quit serving lunches reimbursed under the National School Lunch Program, as two in the Albany area already have done. Several directors bemoaned the trend, which eliminates a program with one real and overriding purpose: to provide children with at least one nutritious meal a day.

Said Alan Muhlnickel, Poughkeepsie food service director, "My staff knows by name the children who come in late on Monday who have had no food all weekend."

When San Francisco schools banned all lunch and snack foods but those on the National School Lunch Program menu, it saw a 27 percent increase in cafeteria meal sales. But school managers locally think that is an extreme measure that would make snack food more desirable while eliminating the chance to educate children on making better choices.

The irony is that schools sell some unhealthy food in order to continue to serve the healthy stuff.

Hyde Park has a color-coded snack-food system—green, yellow and red—to alert children. Pop-Tarts are red; yogurt is yellow; Goldfish crackers are green.

Choose Wisely

Holly Peters Heady, food service manager, said students are told, for example, "If you're going to choose a red-light food, then you have to do X amount of exercise. They have to balance that."

"I don't believe in elimination," she said when asked about school offerings like Choco Taco ice cream. "The chances of binge eating or hiding increase if you take it away totally."

The irony is that schools sell some unhealthy food in order to continue to serve the healthy stuff. The question is how much and of what variety.

Hyde Park, Rhinebeck, Dover, Webutuck and Red Hook follow the "Choose Sensibly" program of the New York School Nutrition Association. Under nonbinding guidelines, snacks should be limited to seven grams or less of fat, 15 grams or less of sugar, 360 milligrams or less of sodium and one serving per package.

Similarly, Poughkeepsie schools follow a 35/35/10 rule of thumb on snacks, stipulating calories should be no more than 35 percent from sugar, 35 percent from fat and 10 percent from saturated fat. Unlike others, the district does not sell Yoo-hoo or Snapple, while chips and popcorn are baked or reduced in fat. None of these districts offer anything near the variety of unapproved foods that Arlington or even Pine Plains, Highland, Millbrook and, to a lesser extent, Spackenkill, Wappingers or Beacon do. (See examples of district menus on www.poughkeepsiejournal.com.)

The release of statistics on overweight and obese children may prompt some soul-searching about the Arlington district menu, Superintendent Brendan Lyons said. Acknowledging that the high school serves fried foods, burgers and other items he called "a temptation" for students, he said, "This is something we have to look at as the expectations of schools change and have changed in playing a larger role in kids' diets. We have to adapt to that."

"Anytime you see that 32.7 percent of our students are in either of those categories (obese or overweight), that certainly doesn't make me feel good. . . . The question is, how can we continue as a school district to work to improve that?"

11

Planting School Gardens
Can Change Students'
Eating Habits

Michele Israel

Michele Israel is the founder of the nonprofit Educational Writing & Consulting and launched a school-garden program in New York City.

Planting school gardens can effectively teach students healthy nutrition and introduce them to food justice issues. Gardening promotes an understanding and appreciation of growing fresh, natural vegetables, which encourages students to change their eating habits and eliminate junk food from their diets. Next, school gardens serve as a platform to explore topics in food, such as sustainability, water conservation, and the advantages of locally grown produce. Some educators may be apprehensive of the costs or may have campuses that lack the capacity for such programs. However, school gardens can be started with simple practices and materials, and schools can team up with food justice organizations to get students involved in extracurricular activities.

Jessica Ramirez, a senior at Balboa High School in San Francisco, was learning about fats when she realized what she usually ate was not doing her much good. "I learned that the decisions I make about what I consume every day have a great impact on my body," says Ramirez.

Then last summer [in 2012], she read *Fast Food Nation: The Dark Side of the All-American Meal*, which hammered home everything she had learned in health class. "My entire view of the fast-food industry changed. I decided to entirely cut out fast food," says Ramirez. Now her goal is to get her family to eat more healthily. "I try to accompany my mom to buy groceries, so she will get more fruits and vegetables, and fewer chips and candies."

Ramirez may not know it, but her food choices have put her at the entry point of the food justice movement. The Brooklyn Food Coalition (BFC), an organization dedicated to creating a just and sustainable food system in Brooklyn, N.Y., defines three key elements of food justice: (1) everyone has a right to healthy, affordable food; (2) food systems should be sustainable; and (3) food workers have a right to fair working conditions.

Beatriz Beckford, BFC's director of organizing and policy and former school food organizing and policy coordinator, believes schools are ripe for the introduction of food justice practices. When young people eat vegetables they've studied in class or grown in a garden, share that experience at home and then request these vegetables at mealtime, says Beckford, they start to probe food's role in their world—just as Ramirez has begun to do.

Start in the Classroom

Introducing students to food justice principles begins in the classroom. Take Balboa High School health teacher Chris Pepper. His ninth-grade health curriculum couples nutrition basics with the study of food origins and preparation. He shows *Food, Inc.*, which gets students talking about animal welfare, industrial agriculture and food workers' rights. His students also research prominent food justice leaders and organizations.

"Teaching about food justice helps make nutrition classes more engaging," says Pepper. "Learning the story of where our food comes from is really interesting, and it involves some real critical thinking about how our world works," he adds.

Vicente Manuel, a former student of Pepper's, has changed his food mindset. "I became aware of the unhealthy foods I was eating," says Manuel. "Now, instead of buying chips, I get fruit. I stopped buying fast food. I eat healthier cooked meals." In the true spirit of food justice, Manuel has urged his mother to change her eating habits, too. He says it's working. She buys more vegetables and fruit and stays away from frozen pre-pared meals and junk food.

School gardens ... have the power to teach young people that access to food can be solved by taking action in one's own community.

School Gardens

National Gardening Association Education Program Coordi-nator Julie Parker-Dickinson is a proponent of teaching food justice through justice-oriented gardening programs. "School gardens," she says, "have the power to teach young people that access to food can be solved by taking action in one's own community."

Say "school garden," and some educators hear "expensive and difficult." But that's not necessarily true. School gardens can start in the simplest of ways.

Steve Ritz, currently dean of students at the Hyde Leader-ship K-12 Charter School in Bronx, N.Y., once accidentally started an indoor garden with his special education students. Ritz had set aside—and forgotten about—a box of daffodil and onion bulbs. When he rediscovered them, several had sprouted. His students forced the rest into bloom on the ra-diator.

"The kids couldn't believe it," says Ritz. "When they realized they could grow things, they wanted to start planting." Thanks to a lot of grow lights, Ritz's classroom at the South Bronx Discovery High School—where he was then teaching—turned into an indoor garden. It produced enough vegetables to contribute to the school cafeteria and send home to families. Students also sold produce at a local farmers market.

Ritz's class went on to build an edible green wall—a self-sufficient vertical garden. Several of his students later became certified in green wall technology, giving them access to employment in the emerging green economy. Students also carried their work into the community by helping a local gardening group clear out a park.

Ritz sees all of this as an excellent model of food justice. "Gardening led to healthy eating and to job development in a new green economy," he says.

Some school gardens, such as the Brooklyn, N.Y., Park Slope Elementary and Middle School's Green Zone, follow a more traditional school garden model. More than 800 elementary and middle school students—60 percent of whom live in poverty—grow herbs and vegetables for the school's lunchtime salad bar. A volunteer nutritionist leads healthy cooking classes, and there is an annual garden-to-school café event.

Schools that don't have the capacity to address food justice issues independently can partner with food justice organizations.

Anita Gasser-Bodzin, Park Slope's Green Zone co-chair, says the program has influenced the way students perceive food. Children first gain an understanding and appreciation of fresh produce that they grow. Then they begin to change their eating habits—in school, at home and beyond.

An understanding of gardening and nutrition is a great start, but school gardens have the potential to serve as a platform for discussions about more complex food-justice issues as well. The Florida-based Bay Haven School of Basics Plus elementary school, for example, uses its school garden project to address agricultural sustainability.

Rolf Hanson, elementary science teacher and coordinator of the Bay Haven garden project, says students use EarthBoxes—sub-irrigated planters that use less water and increase yield—to study issues such as water conservation, organic- vs. petroleum-based fertilizers, pesticide-free gardening and the benefits of locally grown food. The gardening project has changed children's relationship with food. Hanson says his students are excited about gardening, and they're also learning about deeper aspects of food justice.

Organizational Partners

Schools that don't have the capacity to address food justice issues independently can partner with food justice organizations. In this arrangement, schools benefit from outside expertise and resources, and organizations gain access to a youth audience and, sometimes, land on which to grow produce.

Mark Bowen, education and community outreach coordinator at the Montgomery, Ala.-based EAT South, works with children in schools, after-school programs and community-based organizations in poor areas of Montgomery whose residents face food challenges.

Bowen's goal is to introduce children to and excite them about health, nutrition and agricultural sustainability in ways that are mindful of their communities' socio-economic gaps, especially when it comes to the food they eat. "The more kids grow fresh produce," says Bowen, "the more likely they are, as they get older, to break the bad food cycle their parents are in."

In addition to his work with after-school programs, Bowen partners with community-based organizations and schools to model how organic gardening can be done with limited funds by developing gardens using materials that are readily available. (Tires make great planters.) At one elementary school, he helped construct raised beds and a water catchment system and planted fruit trees. He also trains teachers to develop standards-based lessons related to the subjects they teach.

Bowen strongly advises assessing programs to determine what students are learning about food and food systems and if their attitudes toward food are changing. Assessments of EAT South's efforts on the west side of Montgomery showed that students had made measurable gains in their understanding of food origins and the difference between healthy and unhealthy food.

Partnerships also work well in more urban settings. Bushwick Campus High School and EcoStation:NY teamed up to create the Bushwick Campus Farm in Brooklyn, N.Y. The school campus, located in an urban, high-poverty community with above-average rates of diabetes and minimal access to fresh produce in grocery stores and bodegas, is the site of EcoStation's two garden plots, a greenhouse and a water catchment shed.

Classes from the campus' four schools participate in the program, which is incorporated into each school's educational themes. Some students also participate in after-school farm activities, such as nutrition workshops, and in paid summer farm work.

Maggie Cheney, EcoStation's director of farms and education, says the program is committed to involving the entire school community. When students work at the farmers market, says Cheney, they talk with community members about food choices, Supplemental Nutrition Assistance Program (SNAP) benefits that apply to farmers market purchases, food subsidies and discounts on organic produce.

It Can Be Done

It's not hard for students to start exploring and experiencing food justice in school. From making a healthy snack to planting seeds in an indoor garden to watching a film about the agricultural industry, the goal is to get students engaged and excited. That's something a creative educator concerned about students' healthy futures can accomplish—even with very few resources.

12

School Lunches: The New Battlefront in the War Against Obesity

John Dorschner

John Dorschner was a veteran journalist and reporter for the Miami Herald *for more than forty years.*

Students have both negatively and positively reacted to the federal government's strengthening of nutritional standards for school lunches, which emphasize fruits, vegetables, whole grains, low-fat milk, and reducing calories. Some evidence points out that many students are dismayed by the changes, throw away the vegetables, or still consider healthier items "gross." Several student rebellions and boycotts against the standards have also been reported. On the other hand, others observe that food waste by students has not increased since the standards were implemented. And in schools where the switch from junk to healthy foods was an eventual process, students have been generally accepting, with many now making more conscious eating choices.

Around him, many kids in the Sunset Park Elementary cafeteria in South Miami-Dade were gingerly nibbling at fresh vegetables from the new salad bar, encouraged by hovering parent volunteers and teachers. Manuel Rodriguez, 6, had his eyes on something else.

A plastic container, brought from home, contained a thick square of chocolate cake with a layer of white frosting. As he dug into the cake, he was asked if that was all he had for lunch. He shook his head somberly, pointing to a Pedialyte nutrition drink.

With one in three American children considered overweight or obese—and the trend dangerously upward—the federal government has launched a new campaign this school year [2012–2013] to strengthen nutritional requirements for school lunches.

The move has been strongly championed by the White House, particularly first lady Michelle Obama, and it has sparked a backlash. In the politicization of nutrition, Republican stalwart Sarah Palin has defiantly served cookies to children. Conservative talk show host Rush Limbaugh blames the Obamas for destroying Twinkies, while the National Association to Advance Fat Acceptance persuaded Disney World to close down an anti-obesity exhibit.

The larger question is how much a school—or any institution outside the home—can alter eating patterns that many experts believe are deeply ingrained.

Mixed Responses

In the case of school laws, the new standards emphasize fresh fruits and vegetables, whole grains and low-fat milk while limiting caloric intake.

The response, like a serving of succotash, has been mixed.

Many students were dismayed, at least initially. A poll taken by the Coral Gables High newspaper last fall found that 59 percent didn't like the new regulations. Editor Ali Stack said that "students are now used to the food," but miss Papa John's pizza. Overall, she said, attitudes about cafeteria offerings had not changed: "Gross" before and "gross" now.

Sabrina Rodriguez, editor of the Hialeah High newspaper, said most students "still did not like the new standards." They got used to it, she said, but most still throw out the vegetables.

Penny Parham, nutrition director for Miami-Dade schools, said the tales of more waste aren't supported by reports from field offices. In fact, she said increased numbers of elementary and middle school kids are eating cafeteria lunches this year, while high school participation remains about the same. Broward schools also report no waste increase.

The larger question is how much a school—or any institution outside the home—can alter eating patterns that many experts believe are deeply ingrained, starting from the earliest years. Many obesity experts believe changing those habits will take decades. "Note that it took 50 years of anti-tobacco campaigns to lower smoking rates from 50 percent of the population to 20 percent," said James Hill, director of the Center for Human Nutrition in Colorado.

"There's no question that schools can't fix everything," said Roland Sturm, a senior economist specializing in obesity issues at the California-based RAND Corp. Parents' influence remains "hugely important," he said, but "the school environment is an important norm-setter for healthy behavior."

School Menu Changes Bigger in Many Places

With most public school kids in Miami-Dade on free or reduced-lunch programs, and many also eating breakfast, the influence of school menu changes may be bigger than in many places. Still, Sheah Rarback, a University of Miami [UM] nutrition expert, said improving student diets will require "a combined effort to tackle this devastating problem, a real partnership between home and school."

The Barack Obama administration has campaigned to reduce the nation's fat, which has been growing at an alarming rate. The percentage of kids aged 6–11 who are obese has more than doubled in the past three decades, according to the Centers for Disease Control and Prevention. Obese adolescents aged 12–19 have more than tripled. Extra pounds mean extra health problems, such as diabetes and heart disease, adding expense to an industry that already swallows 20 percent of the American economy.

The Healthy, Hunger-Free Kids Act required schools to limit lunches to no more than 650 calories for elementary kids, 700 for middle schoolers and 850 for high schoolers. Students must be offered a vegetable, a fruit, a low-fat or non-fat milk, a protein and a grain. They must pick at least three, one of which must be a vegetable or a fruit. A student also could satisfy the fruit or veggie requirement by choosing a juice without added sugar.

> *It comes down to the individual student. Those who are more health conscious are going to make healthier choices.*

"We're not trying to create waste," said Olga Botero, Miami-Dade schools executive director of food and nutrition.

When the standards kicked in last fall, there were a number of reports of students rebelling at being forced to eat vegetables. The *New York Times* found hundreds of kids in a Wisconsin school boycotting the cafeteria and students in a small town in western Kansas creating a parody video. (In it, athletes keel over in the gym for lack of nourishment and kids stash bags of chips in their lockers to keep from starving.) Even Comedy Central's *The Daily Show* got into the act, showing a New York school waste can overflowing with vegetables.

More Muted Objections

South Florida school nutrition experts say objections were more muted here because there wasn't an overnight switch from junk to healthy foods.

"We've been ahead of this," said Parham, Miami-Dade's nutrition director. "We took off hot dogs last year. It's been quite a while since we served corn dogs. We started whole wheat toast ahead of the requirements." Deep fryers are gone, and so are vending machine sodas.

Darlene Moppert, manager of Broward's nutrition education, said schools there ditched fryers in the 1990s and have offered fresh fruits—bananas, apples and such—for a decade. "It's just that now they're required." She said she's heard few negative comments.

At Cypress Bay in Weston, student journalist Nicole Moshe said her school has "a large amount of students who are very health conscious" and love the fresh fruits and vegetables. She did a survey on the school's food court and found the salad line was as long as those for pizza and hamburgers.

She said "very little" of the fruits and salads are thrown out. "It comes down to the individual student. Those who are more health conscious are going to make healthier choices."

Each county has its own regulations in addition to the federal standards. Broward allows some vendors' products, like pizza, to be sold in some cafeterias, while Miami-Dade no longer permits outside offerings like pizza because companies can't promise to meet healthy guidelines. This year, Miami-Dade also eliminated junk food from vending machines—much to some students' consternation—while Broward still allows some items, like whole grain Pop-Tarts.

Eating Patterns Vary Widely

"I want my Pop-Tarts!" lamented junior Hadiya Trowell at Alonzo and Tracy Mourning High in North Miami as she finished a lunch of brown rice, beef strips and mixed vegetables.

The Mourning vending machines used to be filled with Pop-Tarts and such. Now they're all fresh food—tuna-salad sandwiches and parfait yogurts.

When a Herald reporter and photographer visited Mourning High, kids were in a rush to get their food and eat it during the 30-minute lunch break. For fruits and vegetables, students could pick from whole apples, a box of celery and carrot sticks, hot mixed vegetables, packaged apple slices, strawberry yogurt and several kinds of juices.

Eating patterns varied widely. At one freshmen table, Aubyn Roche had cleaned her plastic plate, including vegetables, while across from her Ariana Aviles hadn't touched her vegetables. "I don't like them," she said flatly.

Roshawn Janvier, a freshman, had chosen a package of apple slices, which remained unopened on his plate after he had finished the rest of the meal. When a reporter asked him if he was going to eat the slices, he said, "Yes!" His buddy Kenneth Gratereaux snorted. "No he's not." Later, as Janvier left the cafeteria, he said he'd eaten "a little" of the apple slices.

While everyone endorses exercise, the value of salad bars remains hotly debated.

At the end of the first lunch shift, the Mourning waste bins contained some vegetables and rice among the plastic dishes, but not a lot.

Rebecca Landesman, a Mourning student journalist, emailed: "From what I see people who buy school lunch will eat the main part of the meal like the chicken or tacos or rice, but they won't eat the fruit and vegetables, which doesn't look as appealing."

But as the school year has gone on, she wrote, "I don't really hear people complaining about it too much anymore. . . . When lunch is over there are dozens of trays left on the tables that have some part of the meal that was left uneaten. Cookies are 50 cents each and they're probably the most purchased food the cafeteria sells."

Teaching nutrition in schools can be a tricky matter. Sturm, the RAND obesity expert, warned that schools can send mixed messages if, for example, they're "using candy or cookies for reward and running for punishment."

He notes that healthier foods alone won't produce thinner kids. Giving kids better nutritional options is a good step, he said, but "don't expect that this magically prevents obesity."

South Florida schools appear to understand that. Miami-Dade has several innovative programs encouraging exercise, even for high school students who don't take regular physical education classes. There's also a program with Miami-Dade Parks and Recreation, promoting after-school exercise programs with healthy snacks—an alternative to flopping on the couch at home and snacking on junk foods while watching TV.

The Debated Value of Salad Bars

While everyone endorses exercise, the value of salad bars remains hotly debated.

Broward schools haven't used salad bars for the past few years because "it's tough to control contamination," said Moppert, the nutrition manager. "And we had a lot of waste." Broward now serves salads in clear plastic containers. In Miami-Dade, salad bars are permitted in schools, when there are enough staff members to control the area, said Parham.

This year, Publix and Produce for Kids, a nonprofit group, have donated 17 salad bars to Miami-Dade schools, including Sunset Park Elementary, where the kids point to the items they want behind a sneeze screen and a cafeteria worker spoons the desired items into a bowl.

At the beginning of the school year, "we had hardly any kids" using the salad bar, said Principal Sara Martin. Then she staged a "tasting day" in which each student was given six little paper cups to sample vegetables and fruits they had never tried before. "They tried it and loved it." And they liked that they could control which items went into the salad. About 250 of the school's 650 students now regularly use the salad bar, Martin said.

"If you start with kindergartners and first graders," said Rarback, the UM nutritionist, "then they're going to be more familiar with fruits and vegetables by the time they're in 11th and 12th grades. I think this process is going to evolve over time."

Organizations to Contact

The editors have compiled the following list of organizations concerned with the issues debated in this book. The descriptions are derived from materials provided by the organizations. All have publications or information available for interested readers. The list was compiled on the date of publication of the present volume; names, addresses, phone and fax numbers, and e-mail and Internet addresses may change. Be aware that many organizations take several weeks or longer to respond to inquiries, so allow as much time as possible.

Campaign for a Commercial-Free Childhood (CCFC)
NonProfit Center, 89 South St., #404, Boston, MA 02111
(617) 896-9368 • fax: (617) 896-9367
e-mail: ccfc@commercialfreechildhood.org
website: www.commercialfreechildhood.org

Founded in 2000, the Campaign for a Commercial-Free Childhood (CCFC) seeks to "reclaim childhood from corporate marketers." Through advocacy and grassroots organizing, it works to limit children's exploitation through commercial culture. Among its many initiatives, CCFC actively discourages marketing in schools, including vending machines and other forms of food marketing. The organization's website offers fact sheets, calls to action, and links to recent news stories.

Center for Science in the Public Interest (CSPI)
1220 L St. NW, Suite 300, Washington, DC 20005
(202) 332-9110 • fax: (202) 265-4954
e-mail: cspinews@cspinet.org
website: www.cspinet.org

The Center for Science in the Public Interest (CSPI) is a consumer advocacy group devoted to funding public policy initiatives as well as scientific research. The organization also works to improve consumer awareness of health and nutrition issues, in large part through a subscription-based magazine (portions of which are available for free online), *Nutrition Action Healthletter*, which includes healthy recipes as well as regular features and analyses of menus at popular restaurants. CSPI's website has a section on "School Foods," which includes a quiz to test users' knowledge of the issue as well as specific suggestions for improving school lunches, snacks, celebrations, and reward programs.

The Edible Schoolyard Project

1517 Shattuck Ave., Berkeley, CA 94709
(510) 843-3811 • fax: (510) 843-3880
website: http://edibleschoolyard.org

Known as the Chez Panisse Foundation until 2011, the Edible Schoolyard Project has the "expanded mission of building and sharing an edible education curriculum for kindergarten through high school." The organization advocates for school lunch reform, in particular the Edible Schoolyard Berkeley, which involves schoolchildren in growing their own food. It also bolsters such programs across the country through its online network and resource center and offers professional development opportunities at its annual Edible Schoolyard Academy. The project's website offers many publications for sale for educators and parents.

Green Schools Initiative

2150 Allston Way, Suite 460, Berkeley, CA 94704
e-mail: info@greenschools.net
website: www.greenschools.net

For the Green Schools Initiative, healthy school lunches are just one facet of an overall approach to healthy, green living at school. Other goals include improving air quality, using natural light, saving energy, creating green schoolyards, and teaching stewardship of the environment. The group's website profiles some schools following its model and offers a set of seven steps schools can follow to easily improve their environments.

It also includes lists of green school products and recommended environmentally friendly industrial cleaners schools can use to keep their environments safe.

Grocery Manufacturers Association (GMA)

1350 I St. NW, Washington, DC 20005
(202) 639-5900 • fax: (202) 639-5932
e-mail: info@gmaonline.org
website: www.gmaonline.org

The Grocery Manufacturers Association (GMA) is the largest trade association for companies making food and beverage products. It channels political contributions, lobbies, and conducts public relations on behalf of its member corporations, which include such multinational companies as Kraft Foods and Pepsi. The association's website provides information about its public policy regarding school nutrition and food marketing.

Healthy School Lunches

5100 Wisconsin Ave. NW, Suite 400
Washington, DC 20016-4131
(202) 686-2210 • fax: (202) 686-2216
e-mail: pcrm@pcrm.org
website: www.pcrm.org/health/healthy-school-lunches

Sponsored by the Physicians Committee for Responsible Medicine, Healthy School Lunches advocates for healthier lunch programs in schools. In particular, the group aims to reduce saturated fat and to increase the amount of plant-based foods in lunches served at schools. The organization's website issues an annual report card on lunch programs at some of the country's largest school districts and offers many other resources.

National Farm to School Network

PMB #104, 8770 West Bryn Mawr Ave., Suite 1300
Chicago, IL 60631-3515
website: www.farmtoschool.org

A project of the Tides Center since 2011, the National Farm to School Network's objective is to connect K–12 schools with local farms with the goal of creating sustainable local school food programs. Overseen by an expanding national and regional infrastructure and staff, the network provides Farm to School programming assistance in all fifty states. It sponsors many local and national events aimed at educating educators, consumers, and administrators about the benefits of locally grown, sustainably produced foods for farmers and for kids. The network's website offers many resources, including educational online videos.

Organic Consumers Association (OCA)
6771 South Silver Hill Dr., Finland, MN   55603
(218) 226-4164
website: www.organicconsumers.org

The Organic Consumers Association (OCA) is an online and grassroots nonprofit organization campaigning for health, justice, and sustainability, dealing with issues of food safety, industrial agriculture, genetic engineering, children's health, corporate accountability, fair trade, environmental sustainability, and other key topics. The organization's website offers links to current news stories, action alerts, and links to other relevant organizations.

Parents Against Junk Food
PO Box 470689, Brookline, MA   02447
e-mail: PAJF@parentsagainstjunkfood.org
website: www.parentsagainstjunkfood.org

Parents Against Junk Food has a straightforward mission: "Stop the sale of junk food in America's schools." Members receive a free e-newsletter and are encouraged to help support anti-junk food legislation in their states. The organization's website includes links to relevant news stories as well as a "Junk Food Hall of Shame," highlighting the poor nutritional choices available to children in America's schools.

US Department of Agriculture (USDA) Food and Nutrition Service (FNS)

3101 Park Center Dr., Alexandria, VA   22302
(703) 305-2062
website: www.fns.usda.gov

The US government's Food and Nutrition Service (FNS) is an agency within the US Department of Agriculture (USDA) that operates a number of food assistance programs for adults and children in the United States, including the National School Lunch Program and the School Breakfast Program. The former is a federally assisted meal program operating in public and nonprofit private schools and residential child care institutions that provides nutritionally balanced, low-cost or free lunches to children each school day. FNS also establishes nutrition standards for school breakfast and lunch programs and is the agency responsible for the Smart Snacks in School guidelines. The FNS website includes links to numerous studies, reports, and fact sheets regarding food nutrition for children and adults.

Yale Rudd Center for Food Policy & Obesity

Yale University, PO Box 208369, New Haven, CT   06520-8369
(203) 432-6700 • fax: (203) 432-9674
website: www.yaleruddcenter.org

The Yale Rudd Center for Food Policy & Obesity seeks to "improve the world's diet, prevent obesity, and reduce weight stigma" through a combination of supporting scientific research and lobbying to improve public policy surrounding these issues. The center's website includes policy briefs and reports, a collection of podcasts featuring noted experts, and links to recent publications about nutrition, food marketing, and obesity.

Bibliography

Books

Kate Adamick	*Lunch Money: Serving Healthy School Food in a Sick Economy.* New York: Cook for America, 2012.
Ann Cooper and Lisa M. Holmes	*Lunch Lessons: Changing the Way We Feed Our Children.* New York: Collins, 2006.
Julie Guthman	*Weighing In: Obesity, Food Justice, and the Limits of Capitalism.* Berkeley: University of California Press, 2011.
Lisa Tillinger Johansen	*Fast Food Vindication.* Los Angeles: J. Murray Press, 2012.
Amy Kalafa	*Lunch Wars: How to Start a School Food Revolution and Win the Battle for Our Children's Health.* New York: Jeremy P. Tacher/Penguin, 2011.
Susan Levine	*School Lunch Politics: The Surprising History of America's Favorite Welfare Program.* Princeton, NJ: Princeton University Press, 2008.
Michael Moss	*Salt, Sugar, Fat: How the Food Giants Hooked Us.* New York: Random House, 2013.
Janet Poppendieck	*Free for All: Fixing School Food in America.* Berkeley: University of California Press, 2010.

| Sarah A. Robert and Marcus B. Weaver-Hightower, eds. | *School Food Politics: The Complex Ecology of Hunger and Feeding in Schools Around the World.* New York: Peter Lang, 2011. |

| Martha Rosenberg | *Born with a Junk Food Deficiency: How Flaks, Quacks, and Hacks Pimp the Public Health.* Amherst, NY: Prometheus Books, 2012. |

| Melanie Warner | *Pandora's Lunchbox: How Processed Food Took Over the American Meal.* New York: Scribner, 2013. |

| Sarah Wu | *Fed Up with Lunch: How One Anonymous Teacher Revealed the Truth About School Lunches—And How to Change Them!* San Francisco: Chronicle Books, 2011. |

Periodicals and Internet Sources

| Ed Bruske | "In DC School Cafeterias, a Long Way from Here to Healthy," *Washington Post*, February 14, 2010. |

| Hank Cardello | "Prohibition: The Wrong Way to Improve Child Nutrition," *Huffington Post*, January 11, 2011. www.huffingtonpost.com. |

| Kathleen Doheny | "Does Junk Food in Schools Matter?," *WebMD*, January 18, 2012. www.webmd.com. |

Food Research and Action Center	"How Competitive Foods in Schools Impact Student Health, School Meal Programs, and Students from Low-Income Families," *Issue Briefs for Child Nutrition Reauthorization*, no. 5, June 2010. http://frac.org.
David H. Freedman	"How Junk Food Can End Obesity," *Atlantic*, July–August 2013.
Simone A. French and Mary Story	"Commentary on Nutrition Standards in the National School Lunch and Breakfast Programs," *JAMA Pediatrics*, January 2013.
Deborah Lehman	"Why School Cafeterias Are Dishing Out Fast Food," Education.com, October 21, 2013. www.education.com.
Timothy D. Lytton	"Why Is There So Much Unhealthy Food in Schools?," *Fooducate*, March 11, 2010. http://blog.fooducate.com.
Anahad O'Connor	"Bans on School Junk Food Pay Off in California," *New York Times*, May 8, 2012. http://well.blogs.nytimes.com.
Joshua Price	"De-Fizzing Schools: The Effect on Student Behavior of Having Vending Machines in Schools," *Agricultural and Resource Economics Review*, April 2012.

Michele Simon   "Ridding Schools of Fast Food, Junk Food, and Soda Pushers," *Food Safety News*, April 8, 2013. www.foodsafetynews.com.

Rodney Taylor, interviewed by Jamie Devereaux   "Salad Bars in Schools," *Childhood Obesity*, August 2012.

Jennifer Warner   "School Vending Machines Still Offer Too Many Sugary Snacks," *WebMD*, February 6, 2012. www.webmd.com.

Index